Fairly Truthful Tales

A collection of comedy monologues
from the North of England

Written and illustrated by
Gary Hogg

Published by
Toontoons

First published in Great Britain by Toontoons 2003

ISBN 978-0-9544794-0-4

British Library Cataloguing in Publication Data.
A catalogue record for this book is available from
the British Library

Printed and bound in Malta for
Compass Press
162-164 Richmond Road, London., SW15 2SL

Published by Toontoons
42 Dunkeld Close
Blyth
NE24 3TA

Website www.garyhogg.co.uk

Contents

(Continued overleaf)

Foreword

It was summer of 2001 when this bloke from near the Arctic Circle sent me one of his monologues - "Dead Men Don't Wear 'erringbone." I thought it was excellent, and set it to music. Thus began the CD collection known as "Fairly Truthful Tales" - stories of the inhabitants of that village called Amblethwaite. We soon had thirteen ready, and the cover was no problem - Gary's an ace cartoonist as well. Now, it takes a certain talent to put a story across in rhyming verses and still make it funny. I'm pleased to say that Gary has an endless supply of this, as can be seen in the content of this book. So, sit down in your favourite chair, turn the telly off, get a cup of tea, or summat with a bit more bant in, and enjoy the wonderous stories from Amblethwaite and Plodgeborough. You might never switch the television back on.

Bernard Wrigley
March 2003

Introduction

Whether it's because the Northern dialect makes comedy sound funnier or Northern humour travels well is yet to be decided. In keeping with tradition and drawing inspiration from the entertainment that packed the halls before television, 'fairly Truthful Tales' hopes to recreate and refresh the art of the comedy monologue.

It was an art form developed in the Victorian Music Halls and artists like Stanley Holloway made it into a working class culture. Young and old in pre-war days memorised their favourites like 'The Lion And Albert,' 'Sam Small' or 'The Runcorn Ferry' and they became a powerful morale booster on the home front during the war. Despite 'Albert' being written by a Scotsman and performed by a Londoner, it was always performed in a Northern accent and fittingly, made its debut in front of a Tyneside audience.

Encouraging older audiences and readers to value their own memories whilst enriching the cultural life of the young, 'fairly Truthful Tales' ensures a vivid part of our comedy heritage is not lost. There is a definite and growing place for this type of entertainment as over a quarter of a million visitors to the 'fairly Truthful Tales' website and others like it, will testify. It's a format that has proved popular with all age groups throughout the Country and overseas and surprisingly, forms part of the English syllabus in some American schools.

Bernard Wrigley was chosen to perform the first collection on CD, his rich Lancashire accent bringing real life and humour to the work. The text has since been cleaned up slightly to enable non-northerners to read it - but feel free to put in the odd 'glottal stop' and drop the odd 'H' as required. Being a Tynesider myself, I decided to do a Geordie version next. The original Geordie texts are even more difficult to understand so they've also been sanitised.

The result is several not entirely accurate accounts of the everyday happenings in Amblethwaite, a small town somewhere up north and to the left – and Plodgeborough, a town slightly further north and nearer the east coast. A bleak and misty range of hills and barren moors separates the pits and shipyards of Plodgeborough from the mills and canals of their neighbours. Somewhere in this void, known to both communities as 'Yon top side,' the dialect changes too. Those in Amblethwaite would say "Up ovver't top side on't bus." Whereas the folks from Plodgeborough would simply "Gan ower yon top side on their bikes"

Not only do you have to travel north but you have to travel backwards to a simpler time. A romantic time when there were mills and shipyards, pits and canals. A time when men thought they were in charge and women were happy to let them (think they were!) It was in times of crisis, some of which are mentioned in these pages, that the strength of the northern woman was evident. The seaside postcard image of the large wife and the tiny henpecked husband was the graphic illustration of this phenomenon.

But don't let me put ideas in your head. Whether reading, listening to the CD or watching a live performance of 'fairly Truthful Tales' the pictures you conjure up in your own head are all yours.

"The CD made me laugh out loud while driving down the M4. Anything that can do that must have a touch of genius"

Alan Plater (Playright)

Acknowledgements

I would like to acknowledge and thank Bernard Wrigley for his inspiration, encouragement and support in the writing and compilation of this book. Also Bill Maynard for his undying enthusiasm and belief in my work. And to friends like Stan Brown, Ray Hooker, Neil Atkinson, Tom McConville, Andrew Peel, George Welsh, Billy Fane, Bill Anderson and Colin & Paul Burke who are responsible for helping to bring the whole process together and knowingly or otherwise planting the seeds from which some of these stories grew.

Front cover photograph of Jimmer Rigg and Johnny McSwain on the village green at Walbottle kindly provided by Mrs L Newton. Published with permission of Newcastle Chronicle and Journal Ltd.

Design: Ian Scott Design

Very special thanks to my wife, Sandra and me Mam.

Dedicated to Fred Burke who wasn't daft.
…well, he was but not much!

The Flight Of Oscar's Undies

It was Monday. It was wash day, and a wind had got up
And you could see that me Mother was itchin'
To get all her washing hung out on the line
'stead of the pulley that hung in the kitchen

"A good drying day is a blessing" she said
Dragging the mangle out into the yard
"Your clothes'll all smell of fresh air for a change,
Instead of them stinking of lard"

Now Mrs Nextdoor lived, well, nextdoor
You'd be kinder to say she was stout
And we'd laugh at the size of her bloomers
On washdays when she had em hung out

Her son Oscar Nextdoor wasn't half a big lad
He longed to be thirteen stone slimmer
But he never really got round to it
Cos he never missed that many dinners

He'd a waistline the size of a coastline
He was just a big dollop of spam
And his underpants were the size of a waste skip
A right struggle to wash for their Mam

She could only fit one pair in the tub at a time
When wet they weighed close on a ton
So she was still pegging stuff out on the line
When others had their ironing done

There was one pair of pants was his favourites
And him not being the sort to wear thongs
These were big belly warming, apple catching, Y fronts
Purple nylon with yellow dots on

It took her six pegs to keep them hung on the line
And with the wind blowing, she had a right job
She had just enough strength left in her, poor lass
To fill the kettle to put on the hob

She just happened to look out the window
And she nearly dropped dead with the fright
Cos there was her Oscar's best Y-Fronts
Setting off over the roofs like a kite

Both ends of the clothesline had pulled themselves loose
And the dogs were all starting to bark
Cos the wind had got into the Y-fronts
Like the mainsail on the old Cutty Sark

Oscar, down his allotment, saw them go past
And he looked and thought "They're just like mine"
Then he realised they were when he saw their back wall
Was still dangling on the end of the line

Now Joby the ragman had just parked his horse
And given it a nosebag of grub
While he negotiated for an old copper boiler
From this wife who'd just bought a twin-tub

He saw the stuff fall, thought his prayers had come true
A whole cartload of clothes from the sky
But the horse, poor lad, he wasn't too pleased
When Oscar's trolleys went 'slap' round his eyes

He showed his annoyance by shaking his head
Then nodding it fast up and down
He went up on his back legs just like Trigger
And belted off down the street towards town

Now Oscar had heard the commotion
And come to see what was the crack
He saw what a state the poor horse was in
And went back for a shovel and sack

Apart from washday, on Mondays, it's the market
The main street fit to bust at the seams
With all sorts of stalls, vans and trailers
And the Walls' bloke selling ice cream

Well the horse just galloped on through there
And stood on a hundred folks' toes
With his lugs sticking out through the leg holes
And the gusset stuck tight to his nose

He was still dragging the clothes-line behind him
And it was collecting all sorts of odd stuff
Like a brolly, a cake stall, and a Walls's bloke
Who, you could see by his face, wasn't chuffed

When the horse reached the end, he'd run out of puff
He'd run out of High street an' all
He crashed through the railings and the big double doors
Of the Amblethwaite and District Town Hall

PC Taylor asked folks what had happened
And started looking around for some clues
The Vicar's wife said "Those pants are Oscar's"
But she blushed when folks asked how she knew

Later that night I was filling the scuttle
When the Police van pulled up at Nextdoors'
They opened the back doors and took out a brick wall
A clothesline and Oscar's best drawers

They said they wouldn't be pressing no charges
It had been a fluke, act of God, so to speak
But Oscar was still quite embarrassed
And didn't show his face for three weeks

They still talk of the day that his undies took flight
And some folk can be a bit mean
But Mrs Nextdoor can still hold her head high
At least the underpants involved had been clean

The Bartholomew Family Photograph

When Mrs Bartholemew come in from the shops
She said to their Dad, "Listen Joe,
I've just been and booked to get a photograph took,
It's on special, just a guinea a go"

"A guinea?" said Pa, she says "Aye. Innit cheap?"
He says "Cheap? I could do it for nowt"
"You're hopeless" she said, "You always chop off our heads,
Else our lugs's got trees sticking out"

She says "He's coming at two and there's plenty to do,
So we haven't got long. Shake a leg!"
Pa let out a groan, she says "Go and get our Joan,
And tell her to fetch Tommy and Peg"

She took the newspaper off the parlour table
The ration books from the back o' the clock
A picture of the Town Hall over the hole in the wall
How she wished that her pearls weren't in hock

She says "Get yer teeth, have a shave while you're on,
Aye, and put a clean collar on too,
Roll them cuffs out of sight, and put yer hair right"
Says Pa "What a bloody to-do"

She says "Make sure our Tommy puts on his nice tie,
While I go and slap on some glamour,
And make sure number one's got her uniform on,
Folks should know she's at Amblethwaite Grammar"

"And make sure she's wearing her monitor's badge
I'm proud of our Peg, so I am,
I've got some fruit for that bowl, get a shovel of coal,
And put some Schubert on the radiogram"

She shifted the rent book off the top of the mantle
So's folks might think the house was their own
She then started pushin' magazines under cushions
And Pa had to shift his trombone

Then he rounded the kids up like mother had said
And got them all in the parlour right quick
But they'd mud on their knees and Joan needed a wee
And Tommy's face could've done with a lick

Pa put on a fresh collar and his funeral tie
As Ma stood there looking quite chic
"I'm not paying a guinea to be seen in me pinny"
Says she, putting rouge on her cheeks

Then she stood on a chair and reached up with the mop
To get a cobweb from the top of the door
Joan swept the grate, Tommy shifted his skates
While Peg pushed the brush round the floor

"I want this here rug pulled into the corner,
So folks think we've got wall-to-wall,
And we can't have them woollies hung up on that pulley,
Stick 'em on the clothes-horse out there in the hall"

"Can Patch get his picture took too?" said Young Joan
"He'll just bark and spoil it" says Peg
"No he won't," "Yes he will," "No he won't," "Yes, he will"
Then Peg nipped the back of Joan's leg

Then Joan started crying and her eyes went all red
And the dog started barking like mad
So Joan fetched their Peg a good slap round the head
Then they both got a smack from their Dad

"Stop teasing" said Mother giving Pa a quick dig
"And get a garter for our Joan's sock"
Peg says "It's too late, he's just come in the gate"
And just then they heard the bloke knock

"Quick, all of you, get stood in this corner" says Ma
"Open the door Pa, he's not got all day"
Pa scratched his head, "Make your mind up!" he said
"Do you want us to go or to stay?"

"Oh, I'll go!" says Ma "You'll just get in a mess,
You just come and get stood standing here,
It's no beauty spot but it's the best that we've got,
And it was only distempered last year"

She opened the door for the photographer, Mr McGuire
Saying "Do come in" in a voice proper swanky
Pa was still in his slippers so he stood behind the nippers
And wiped their faces wi' spit on his hanky

The photographer looked and said "Oh, this looks nice"
He says "I hope you haven't gone to no bother"
Pa nearly let slip, then he buttoned his lip
When he saw the expression on mother

"The lengths some folks go just to put on a show"
Said the photographer, looking at Pa
But Pa'd nowt to say 'case he gave the game away
"Oh, you just take us as you find us" says Ma

The Day That Tim Sykes
Packed In Talking

Tim Sykes, rest his soul, just wouldn't shut up
He's talked many's a glass eye to sleep
And somewhere he must have a collection
Of donkeys' hind legs in a heap

He could talk for an hour on nothing at all
Like the ration book his sister once lost
Or the day that the bread van was twelve minutes late
As if any of us give a toss

So most folks avoided Tim, best as they could
Not cos there was anything wrong
He'd a heart of gold, Tim, but like Fred Burke once said
"He's a good turn, he just stays on too long"

He was a steeplejack by trade and a good one, I'm told
Worked alone, well most of the time
But he'd yap on to anyone he caught walking past
No matter how high up he'd climbed

He caught me one day, I hadn't a clue
If I'd known I'd have hid double quick
But me head was down dodging the puddles
And he was fifty foot up on Saint Nick's

He shouts "Hey up there Bill, nice weather for ducks,
Not so good for us poor steeplejacks"
He shouts "Do you think that it's going to stop raining?"
"Well it usually does," I shouts back

Too late, he got on about raincoats
The best part of an hour I was trapped
He moaned at the price of tea during the war
I got a crick in me neck while he yapped

He was fitting a lightning conductor
On the spire of Saint Nic's C of E
If a church needs a lightning conductor
What chance for poor sinners like me?

That was the last time I saw poor Tim Sykes alive
Cos it wasn't too long after that
He got a job on some scaffolding ninety foot up
On the top of them new multi-flats

It was the light at the top that had gone on the blink
So they sent Tim on up to re-wire it
He made such a good job, he got carried away
Daft bugger stepped back to admire it

Now apart from a plank there was nowt but fresh air
He inadvertently fell ninety foot
He was spread thinner than Marmite in wartime
And his bait box and flask were kaput

But he'd wanted to die with his boots on
Cos there was always big holes in his socks
So he shouldn't have been disappointed
But it still might've come as a shock

He was laid out at home in the parlour
In his blazer, medals pinned to his chest
His wife May looked down at him sadly and said
"Least his teeth'll be getting a rest"

You talk about long suffering spouses
Forty years May put up wi' old Tim
It was a blessing I suppose, she was deaf in one lug
The one that she kept nearest him

So there was quite a few there at the funeral
To pay our respects to poor Tim
It was the first time we'd been in his company
And able to get a word in

Mr McSomething was the vicar they'd got
He says "We're here to celebrate the life,
Of our dearly departed Septimus Sykes"
"Din't know that was 'is name" says his wife

'Course the vicar, poor lad, hardly knew him at all
And he spoke full of graces and airs
About what a quiet soul our poor Tim had been
Mind, that vicar says owt but his prayers

He said things like "Reserved" and "A man of few words"
And when he was saying his final 'Amen'
I couldn't believe it, I turned to me mate
I says "Whose funeral is it again?"

And afterwards at the house was a quiet affair
There was no-one would open their gob
We were all sat around, I must say, lost for words
We were that used to it being Tim's job

Then eventually I came up with something
"He's at peace now" I says to his May
She says "It's us lot, at last, that'll be getting some peace,
Without that bugger prattling all day!"

The Angel Down The Allotment

Norm was down the allotment planting some spuds
A dirty great angel appeared out of thin air
Norm says "Watch where you're putting your stupid big feet,
I've got two rows of onions in there"

The angel says "Give us a chance, pal. Don't lose your rag,
I've pulled a muscle in one of me wings,
So me landing technique has all gone to cock,
And I've dropped all me papers and things"

Norm says "Pass me that hoe, I'll have to re-do that row,
It's back breaking, is this, by myself,
Do you know how much digging and weeding it takes?
You think I'm here for the good of me health?"

The Angel says "Stop yer bleatin' and give us a break,
Can you not see that I'm in a bad way,
You want to try living life as an angel,
I'd do yer a swop anyday"

So Norm says "I'm sorry, sit yourself down,
There's a cup of hot tea in me flask"
The angel said "Don't s'pose you've got a spare fag?"
Well you never get nowt less you ask

So they had a quick fag and a hot cup of tea
The angel started to look through his notes
He says "Right Norm, to business, now lets have a look,
How are y'on for building us a boat?"

Norm says "Boat?" He says "Aye, you not done one before?"
Norm says "No. Have I hell. Why? Have you?"
He says "Well no, I'm an angel there isn't much call,
But your gonna need one down here pretty soon"

"You've been given a job, see. You've to build a big ark,
And it's says here you haven't got long"
Norm says "Eh? Are you sure?" He says "Aye, it sez here"
He says "Give ower you must have it wrong"

"It's here in me notes - Three hundred cubits in length,
Gopher wood, pitched within and without,
Then there's a big list of animals you've got to collect,
If you're stuck you can give us a shout"

Norm says "Don't be so daft, I'm a pitman by trade,
Building a boat's gonna be pretty hard,
And what the hell's this about cubits?
What's a cubit? A nautical yard?"

"I'm buggered if I know" the angel replied
Being polite, then he says "Any road….,
It says on me list you're an ark wright, look here,
N. Arkwright, it says, Ropeworks Road"

Then he says "Damn, it's not you it's your missus I want,
Norah's her name, am I right?"
Norm says "Aye," he says "Good, has she got any wood?
And do you know if she's doing owt tonight?"

"Not Norah the ark-wright, you daft ha'porth," says Norm
"She's an Arkwright, but that's just our name"
Then the angel says "Norm, is she an Arkwright or not?
I haven't got time for no games"

"I'll 'no-time-for-games' you, in a minute" says Norm
"There's no need to get all high and mighty,
Who's the one playing games, you daft seagull?
It's not me that's stood here in a nightie"

"Yes, she's an Arkwright, you need to wash out your lugs,
And between you and me and the cat,
I've got serious doubts, cos I'll tell you for nowt,
Norah won't go a bundle on that"

Well at this the angel got a bit of a lip on
He says "Look, who's the angel round here?
If I say your lass's got to build a big boat,
Then she'll build a big boat, is that clear?"

"You're not listening" said Norm "Yes I am" "No you're not,
I might as well talk to that tree,
She's her bingo tonight, so she'll put up a fight,
Are you gonna tell her or me?"

Then he grabbed at the list and he started to laugh
As he looked up their name on the sheet
He says "Look, for God's sake, you've a typing mistake,
You want Noah, the old bloke down the street"

"He's a dab hand wi' boats is old Noah" says Norm
Picking up his spade once again
"In the time we've been stood, I could've planted these spuds,
And now look, it's bloody starting to rain!"

A Funny Thing Happened On The Way From The Crem.

We cremated old Bert the March afore last
We had to, he'd been dead for a week
Fell in the canal and got frozen. Not the end he'd've chosen
But he was thawed out eventually, so to speak

Old Billy come knocking, he'd heard nowt of the death
There's young Polly, full of emotion
She says "We've just lost me Dad" Bill says "My, that is sad,
But did he say owt about a tin of emulsion?"

Well, you don't know what to say, on the spot, sort of style
He could see that she'd been in the wars
Says "You must feel so numb, like when we lost our Mum,
She's somewhere in British Home Stores!"

Now a few years beforehand Bert's Annie had said
"When the subject of dying arises,
D'you want buried at Benton? or cremated at Denton?"
He just looked and he whispered "Surprise us"

All his cronies turned up, half past two at the Crem
It was lovely to see 'em all there
In their scarves and long-johns, with their woolly hats on
It was the coldest day of the year

I caught sight of Seth Butcher, he didn't look grand
Doesn't get out much on account of his gout
I says "Hey up there, Butch." He says "Weather's not much"
I says "No, but it's better than nowt"

"How old was he then?" says Jimmy McNabb
"He was ninety last week" says our Pat
"That's no age" he said, I says "No but he's dead,
You don't get much older than that"

Not a bad turn out considering the day
And the hymns that they sung, they were nice
But the big problems come when they tried to get home
The cortege went and stuck on the ice

It had snowed for six weeks then turned into slush
On the day of the funeral it froze
They pushed Annie's car first, they swore and they cursed
It took them a good four or five goes

The lads' car was next and they pushed and they shoved
But the wheels just continued to slip
The Crematorium man, Joe, says "If you hang on a mo,
You can have some ashes to give you more grip"

Course, when they got going, Joe runs alongside
"D'you want this urn then?" he shouts, to young Jim
"The bill's all been paid, so it's yours I'm afraid,
But I'm sorry, there's bugger all in"

So Jim grabbed the urn, says "I know what we'll do,
Mam'll know right away 'cos it's light,
Get some ash from the bin, just in case she looks in,
And we'll screw down the lid extra tight"

Annie had aired the front parlour, put fruit in the bowl
A bottle of sherry was stood on the dresser
She'd borrowed some chairs and swept the back stairs
She'd even hung up Bert's photograph, bless her

'Course, she got home first, she put on a brave face
And she smiled as she welcomed the lads
She says "Eeh, I'm all in. Pour us a gin,
Then we'll have a quick look at your Dad"

She spread yesterday's newspaper out on the floor
The lads looked but they dared to say nowt
Then poor Jim went and hid when she unscrewed the lid
And carefully emptied it out

She says "Would you believe it, that's all there's to show,
Eighteen stone and as tall as a prop,
And now me poor Bert, you're just a handful of dirt,
An eggshell and a milk bottle top"

The Mystery Of The Boating Lake Mermaid

When Alec came into the pub Thursday night
We knew there was summat going on
He hadn't been shaved, I don't think he'd slept
And his mac was all buttoned up wrong

He says "I think I saw a mermaid last night in the park,
Strangest thing that I've ever seen,
I don't think I was drunk" he said, ordering a Coke
Just in case he might just could've been

Well all his mates sat around, their gobs open wide
As Alec sat and loosened his scarf
He took a sip of his Coke and started to choke
And had to go back to the bar for a half

He'd been taking a shortcut through Amblethwaite park
Last night, having had one or two
And he found him a tree just to have a quick pee
Just to lighten the load, like you do

"I was just by the boating lake there in the dark,"
He says "Looking out to the isle in the middle,
And I saw this young mermaid wriggling about,
And giving her tail a bit twiddle"

"What the hell did you do?" said his mate Arthur Clegg
Through a mouthful of ham and egg pie
"What could I have done? I just cut and I run,
I don't think I even buttoned me fly"

So his mate Bert McGarr says "Just calm yourself down,
And we'll see if we can sort this one out"
He says "Here's what we'll do, why don't we all come too?
'Course it's not that we doubt you, or nowt"

So it comes half past ten and they assembled outside
There was Arthur and Bert and Stan Stokes
And Big Ray and his mate and a couple of crates
Alec and Seth and the Sally-Ann bloke

They crossed over the road and climbed through the fence
And silently made their way through the park
Black as inside a bull's gut with its tail down, it was
Not a nice place at all in the dark

It was quite eerie in there in the dead of the night
They'd to toss to see who should go first
With the wind going wooo in the leaves round their heads
And an owl giving a hoot made it worse

They got down to the jetty where the boats were tied up
And they found themselves somewhere to sit
And the boats gently rocked on the ripples
And give a bit clunk when they hit

"She's not there," said Stan "We might as well go"
He wasn't too keen on the place
Then he heard this bit rustle and tensed all his muscles
As a kebab paper flew up in his face

Then they all heard a twig snap behind them
And a deep sort of bronchial cough
And there stood this dark figure with a boat hook
"The boats are closed for the night, Bugger off!"

Now despite the figure's sinister demeanour
His black clothes and a shiny peaked cap
And a great big long pole with a hook on
He seemed a reasonable sort of a chap

Bert thought that he'd best just explain things
And he offered him a bottle of beer
And he said "You'll n'arf laugh when we tell you,
Why us lot are sat sitting here"

"You see Old Alec here, though he might be mistaken,
Was walking this way just last night,
And he saw what he thought was a mermaid,
So we thought, if we came, then we might"

The bloke took a deep breath and then he let out this laugh
And it echoed loud all round the park
And a poor wood pigeon who'd been trying to kip
Flew off saying "Sod this for a lark"

The boatman calmed down, he said "I know what you saw,
It was nothing to give you a scare,
You saw young Bessie Stokoe from Bolingbroke Street,
Cos I saw her meself, I were there"

"I'd chased her and her boyfriend when I locked up the park,
They were snogging on the park's bowling green,
Running her hands through his hair like a Nit Nurse, she was,
I could see they were building up steam"

"So they must've sneaked back and untied a boat,
And set off to the island for more,
Cos I was doing me rounds at this time last night,
And they were giving it six-nowt on the shore"

"Then they saw me and they seemed to lose interest,
Cos you know Knuckles Stokoe, her Dad?
Hairs on his teeth and tattoos on his eyeballs?
Well they know I play darts with the lad"

So it wasn't a mermaid that Alec had seen
It was Bessie and her lad taking flight
She was in such a flap, that she had a mishap
And got both feet down one leg of her tights

Dead Men Don't Wear Herringbone

I remember when old Alfred Stone popped his clogs
He was taken to the chapel of rest
He was wearing the clothes that he'd died in
His moleskins and a raggy string vest

The undertaker, Stan Stokes from the Co-op
Being respectful but still quite astute
Had a quick look in the wardrobe
And grabbed Alfred's blue de-mob suit

Stan did a good job on old Alfred
Trimmed the hairs from his nose and his ears
In his suit, with three fingers of Brylcreem
He looked better'n he had done in years

Old Peggy got on with the mourning
And whilst going through Alfred's effects
Was overcome with a sudden compulsion
To go and pay final respects

The chapel of rest was just closing
When the Amblethwaite bus got to town
Stan Stokes was putting the bolt in the door
And starting to pull the blinds down

He saw Peggy and, being respectful
Said "Come in, Pet. Sit yourself down,
But could you be in and back out in ten minutes?
I've a darts match tonight at the Crown"

He showed her through the back-shop to the chapel
And, respectfully, lifted the top
He left her stood at the side of the coffin
And went back to sit in the shop

He'd just put his feet on the pot-bellied stove
When Peggy come rushing back through
He got such a fright, set his turn-ups alight
And, respectfully, shouts "What's to do?"

She says "Nowt's wrong my pet, 'fact he looks really well,
You've done a grand job, he looks cute,
Just he's been saying for years, when he gets to the gates,
He wants to be wearing his Herringbone suit"

Stan says "There isn't much time to do owt,
The funeral's tomorrow at two,
Me assistant's been off for a week with his neck,
I'll promise nowt, but I'll see what I can do"

So Peggy went home and Stan went to his darts
They got hammered by the lads from the Swan
"It's me mind" says poor Stan "It's just not on the game,
I keep thinking what Alfred's got on"

Peggy called at the Co-op next day about noon
Just to have a last look at her Love
Stan had this big smile, he says "I think you'll be chuffed"
Peggy looked and said "Heavens above!"

And there lay old Alf in a Herringbone suit
She says "How the hell d'you do that?"
Stan whispered and says "I bent some of the rules,
You'll have to keep it under your hat"

"It was a coincidence, you see, but I got this lad in,
And just as I put on the top,
I noticed the Herringbone suit he had on,
And I thought I'd perhaps do a swap"

"So I measured their heights, they were both five foot two,
They were even the same inside leg,
So not to disturb them any more than was right,
Respectfully, I just swapped their heads"

Edie's Last Ride

She was a lovely old lass was Aunt Edie
And it fair brings a tear to me eye
'Cos she had such a passion for living
You'd think the last thing she'd do was to die

She was fit as a lop was old Edie
And was always so kind and polite
Doing favours and shopping for neighbours
On the go from morning till night

The sea air, she'd said, had been good for her health
She took it in every day in deep breaths
In fact, the folks of the town were so healthy
The undertaker, poor lad, starved to death

When she got into her nineties she started to slow
She always said it would happen one day
She was put in a wheelchair, 'cos her legs were no use
Well, no use as legs anyway

But she still got about as best as she could
There was nothing would hold the lass back
All her dusting was done when the home help got there
And she'd even been round with the vac

She used to bowl herself out and sit at the gate
She was fond of her yackety-yack
She would talk to the folks on their way to the shops
And then catch them all on the way back

She was famous in Amblemouth, Edie
There was some people one day walking past
They said "You must be the oldest inhabitant?"
She says "No, he died the year afore last"

She was a mine of information was Edie
She remembered things most would forget
I said "Have you lived in Amblemouth all of your life?"
She said "No Pet, I haven't, ...not yet"

One Monday at her lunch club up at the Mem.
In her wheelchair on account of her knees
It was roast lamb and Jersey potatoes
Mint sauce and a few garden peas

They had best butter to put on their taties
She says "Oooh thanks" and took a big pat
But she dropped some on the brakes of her wheelchair
She went down hill pretty quick after that

It was just when they lifted her out of the bus
And she was getting her key from her pocket
The man set her down on the path by the gate
But she shot off down the bank like a rocket

With her front wheels in the air like a dragster
Nowt to sixty in six seconds flat
With one hand trying to pull on the brake thing
And the other hanging on to her hat

She was heading for the newsagent's window
Young Norman was out washing the sign
He shouts "Your People's Friend isn't in yet"
"That's okay," she shouts, "Some other time!"

She spat on her hand and slowed down the left wheel
She swerved under his ladder with skill
She shouts "It's a good job I'm not superstitious"
And accelerated off down the hill

There was a tyre-mark round the bend by the pork shop
And another up Wilkinson's cat
A scrape down the Mobile Library
And a hedgehog, poor bugger, squashed flat

She swerved in and out of the traffic
Getting good at this cornering lark
But she still couldn't stop, she went up the grass verge
Crossed the A1 and into the park

They found her face down in the duck pond
And they think she must somehow have flown
'Cos her wheelchair was stuck in the railings
She'd done the last fifty yards on her own

So that's the sad tale of Aunt Edie
But she wouldn't want loved ones to weep
Thoughtful to the end, cos at this time of year
You can get a big bunch of flowers quite cheap

When You've Had Yer Chips

There's a chip shop on Plodgeborough High Street
That's owned by a bloke called Jed Craddock
I was in Sunday night on me way from the pub
I forget what I got - probbly Haddock

As usual, it's not ready so I sat down to wait
And I had a bit natter to Jed
He says "Taties have gone up to a shilling a pound,
Oh, and Joe Pringle the milkman's dropped dead"

I was shocked I said "Never!" He said "Aye" I said "No!"
I had to sit down, I said "When?"
He says "Starting today they're a shilling a pound"
I said "What price'll four penn'orth be then?"

"They'll have to be sixpence by my workings out,
And that's still eating in to me profits"
I says "Well I'll have to cut down to just five nights a week,
Cos when I tell our lass she'll go off it"

It was next morning I remembered Joe Pringle
When I was raking the back of the grate
And how Jed had said like he'd snuffed it
To be fair, I had been in a state

He was a lovely old lad was Joe Pringle
The sort of man you don't meet every day
Unless'n of course he's your milkman n'that
Which he was, so you would, I dare say

They weren't regular churchgoers, the Pringles
Not cos they were heathens nor nowt
Just they never seemed to get round to it
Well not until Joseph pegged out

The Minister called round the day after he died
"Ah, your Worship, come in" says Irene
And she showed him through into the parlour
Where Joe was laid out all serene

She'd lit a few candles, she didn't know why
She'd seen it one time on TV
And the vicar said a prayer and blessed him and that
And then she poured him a nice cup of tea

He had a sip, then he says "What hymns did he like?"
"Well I don't really know" says Irene
She thought for a while then she says with a smile
"The Northern Lights of Old Aberdeen?"

The Vicar, Mr Hardy was a miserable sod
And he thought it an utter disgrace
And he gave her a look like she'd farted in church
Like they'd dropped a stitch when they knitted his face

"That's not really a hymn," he explained with a sigh
He could see that she hadn't a clue
But she wouldn't be phased, "He liked Songs of Praise,"
She says "The Old Rugged Cross, that'll do"

"I'll pick the hymns, eh?" the Minister says
"Well if you're sure you don't think it's a cheek,
And do you mind if we have him cremated,
I can't be on wi' going visiting each week"

Then he gave her a lecture about dying and stuff
And he talked for three quarters of an hour
All about life and death and resurrection and that
And God and his almighty power

He said God had made everything on this here earth
And she agreed that he probably had
Well that's all excepting the shed in the yard
It was Joe what built that with his Dad

He said that though Joe was still here in body
His spirit was in a far nicer place
And she thought right enough he'd be up there
Just starting to unpack his case

And she wondered a while how he was settling in
And if he'd be feeling okay
She thought "That's the worst of being dead, sort of style,
You must feel a bit stiff the next day"

And right enough at that time, Joe was sat on a cloud
Having a crack with some of his mates
Them what had died a few years afore
He was bringing them all up to date

Wi' the happenings of Plodgeborough since they'd been gone
They wanted to know all the gen
And a few of 'em got a bit homesick
Hearing who'd been doing what, where and when

But despite all their tearful reminiscence
His stories just served to compound
A general consensus they were in the right place
Specially wi' taties at a shilling a pound!

A Job Well Done

My eighth birthday we'd a party at our house
With seventeen kids from my class
We had charades and cheese scones and jelly
And a man came to cut off the gas

Now me dad, like you know, was deaf in one lug
'Cut the grass' is what he thought he'd said
It was 'Bob-a-Job' week and Dad being generous
Said "Okay, bonny lad, go ahead"

He'd a long mac smelt of stagnant old floorcloths
He didn't look nowt like a scout
And he didn't have short pants or a beret
No badges or a woggle or nowt

He went into the cupboard under the stairs
Me Dad was puzzled but said "Mind your head,
If you're looking for the mower we've not got one,
You'll have to use clippers instead"

The bloke seemed to manage with the tools that he had
A pair of pliers and a big rusty spanner
And me dad reached deep in his pocket
And give him a couple of tanners

It was when me Mam went to make me Dad's dinner
That she noticed the gas wasn't on
Cos the chips were still white after nearly an hour
So he had to have jelly and scones

And when he complained me mother went mad
I thought she was going to kill
She smacked me Dad round the head with the chip pan
Cos it was his job to pay all the bills

The next morning I got up for me paper round
I couldn't get through the back door
Cos me Dad lay with his head in the oven
And his legs stretched all ower floor

I had to climb over and squeeze meself in
Cos he hadn't left us much space
And I got him a pillow to put under his head
Cos he was getting a ridge on his face

I'd to help me Mam make the dinner
When I got back from school that night
She was still in a huff on account of the gas
And me Dad, 'course, was nowhere in sight

Me Mam was heating up peas in the kettle
And I had to stand up a height
And I was browning the top of a big shepherds pie
By holding it under the light

After tea me Mam sat on the piano stool
In the corner where the piano once stood
Humming Rachmaninov's piano concerto
In as close to C minor as she could

It was then that we noticed the piano had gone
Cos it should have been stood standing there
Dad says "I've sold it and paid that daft gas bill"
She says "Well I'll go to the foot of our stairs!"

He says "Don't get yer liberty bodice in a twist,
It's at the pawnshop on Bolingbroke Street,
I'll be straight back up there on payday"
And he proved it by showing the receipt

She got up from the stool in a temper
Like she was going to thump him some more
Cos she picked up her banjo by the thin end
But he was saved by a knock at the door

It was the bloke in the mac with the pliers stood there
And me dad thought 'By, this Boy Scout's willing'
He says "You see if you can sort out the gas, son,
And I'll see if I can find you a shilling"

So that evening was all peace and quiet
With me Mam and me Dad just sat there
Listening to Billy Cotton on the wireless
Then suddenly, dad jumps out his chair

He says "That bloody Boy Scout's an impostor!
I've just been sat here working out,
That bugger's done me for two shillings,
And I didn't get a sticker nor nowt!"

The Secret Life Of Walter's Mittens

There was a jumble sale at Amblethwaite Scout Hut
Not last Sunday, Sunday before
And our Walter knew, He'd be first in the queue
He took a flask and camped out at the door

He woke up on the step the next morning
With damp trousers, stiff neck and back ache
He'd to make sure to get back his belongings
That their Mam gave away by mistake

He wasn't bothered about the Broons book or bike pump
Or his clothes or the rest of the clutter
It was his old woolly mitts, all holey and split
That were making him behave like a nutter

He paid the Scoutmaster ninepence to get the mitts back
He thought Walter was out of his head
Paying that for some raggy old mittens
But he'd've paid him ten bob if he'd said

You see the mitts had been knit by his Grandma
From an old Persian rug she'd unravelled
It was an ugly old matted-up eyesore
That Grandpa'd picked up on his travels

Nobody knew that the carpet was magic
He'd picked it up in some distant bazaar
When he was travelling the world with a circus
As a clown. Are you with me so far?

Now nobody knew of its powers or owt
And Grandpa himself is long gone
In fact we don't even know if he'd give it a go
If he had, well, he'd never let on

You see magic carpets are a tad temperamental
And you need to say 'Alacazam'
But if nobody told you, you'd likely not know
So it just sat on the floor at his Gran's

But its powers passed on to the mitts, wi' the wool
But still no one knew what was what
Until one day last March when young Walter
Put the mitts on to go to the shop

Cos Walter was an apprentice in the garage, you see
In the back lane behind the Co-op
And in keeping with motor-trade traditions
At dinner times got sent to the shop

Now one day his list got blown out of his hand
But don't worry - all the blokes still got fed
Cos he'd a dead good memory, had Walter
He could recite it off the top of his head

"Ray always has cheese and Duffy has egg,
And a bacon and brown sauce for Jimmy,
And Billy has Spam and Alec-has-ham"
'Course he'd said magic word. Are you wi' me?

I told you, 'Alacazam' was the mystical word
That would bring the magic carpet to life
Or at least it would have had it not been unravelled
To make mitts by some silly old wife

There was a funny sensation occurred in his mittens
Poor Walter was quite overcome
"This is the magic carpet but I'm not promising nowt"
Said a voice from a hole in the thumb

"Oh, Aye?" says young Walter, dubious like
Well, you would if your mitts started talking
It caused quite a stir to poor Walter stood there
And all the folks in the shop stood there gawkin'

"You are my master"said the voice from within
"Just say where you'd like me to fly,
Though it might be a bit tricky on account of me shape"
Said the mitts "But I'll give it a try"

"We could go to the Cup Final but that's not till May"
Says young Walter scratching his ear
"Cup Final? Fine, we can travel through time,
It's been dead boring this last fifty year"

So they soared off up over the roof tops
They were at Wembley in a couple of ticks
I'll not tell you who won 'case it spoils it
But he was happy that his team scored six

Now the mitts picked him up and brought him back home
To the garage where the lads were stood round
Saying "Where the hell have you been for our sarnies?
And what you doing three foot off the ground?"

So Walter told them the tale of the mittens
And how he'd said the magic word in the shop
"So what was it you said, then?" - says Alec
"I'm buggered if I know. I forgot"

"It'll likely be abracadabra"
Said Ray who knew nowt about owt
And they spent the rest of the day on suggestions
But managed to come up with nowt

Though he'd been to Wembley and back in ten minutes
The ham went off during the flight
And poor Alec got food poisoning for his trouble
And had déjà vu with the sarnie that night

But Walter still hopes as he goes for their dinners
That one day he might get a repeat
But he's not likely to say 'Alacazam' any more
Alec's turned Veggie and give up on meat!

A Pale Brew Yonder

I was coming back from our Jessie's last Tuesday
On the fell road up ower the top
There's an old single-decker selling hot dogs and teas
So I thought that I'd mebbe just stop

"Have you booked?" says the bloke, with a fag in his gob
And a squint in one of his eyes
I says "Less of your cheek, I'll have one of yer teas,
And one of them things looks like pies"

I took a seat at this formica table
That was swimming in puddles and crumbs
And he slopped down this blue and white mug full of tea
And held me pie on the plate with his thumb

It was a typical greasy spoon hovel
And in the middle o' the table of course
There was one of them plastic tomatoes
For them folks what likes a bit sauce

I never said nowt I just took a quick sip
And you know it wasn't too bad
In fact it's a serious contender
For the best cup of tea that I've had

It was just the right strength, not too weak, not too stewed
The right colour and temperature too
And I just got to thinking, how come our Jess
Has such trouble in making a brew

It's good water ruined is a cup of her tea
It won't stain the cloth it's so weak
You see tea needs to sit and calm itself down
Pull itself together, so to speak

I've got through some tea in my lifetime
So I think that I stand well equipped
To say what I think about quality
Of the beverage that passes me lips

I've had afternoon teas, I've had high teas
In tea rooms and hotels and caffs
So I think that I know what tastes proper
But our Jessie? She's having a laugh

In the army us lads had to make do with tea
Brewed up in all sorts of manner
A billy-can, no handle, all dirty and black
And stirred with a five-sixteenths spanner

With a dirty great oil slick floating on top
And a few lumps of grass was the norm
A variety of bugs doing the breaststroke
But at least it was served wet and warm

Or a twice brewed concoction made over a fire
Boiled up in a mucky tin hat
A teaspoonful of milk to share between three
You can't get more desperate than that

But then you haven't sampled our Jessie's
Despite her and her bone china pot
It's not even near the right colour
About three leaves per cup, like as not

I dread when I hear her come out with the words
"I'll make us a nice pot of tea"
She made us Earl Grey the last time I was there
Tart's bathwater if you ask me

I've had a lifetime of just grin-and-bear-it
I've been going there ever since I was nine
But one day I'll pluck up the courage
To say "Make mine a coffee this time!"

It's No Life Being Dead

Now when old Eric Stobbs turned a hundred and six
His welcome, he felt, was outstayed
At the gates he was knocking, and mind, he looked shocking
So he thought about calling it a day

He was thinking of turning his toes up
His clogs were about ready for popping
If he wasn't so lazy he'd be pushing up daisies
Off the twig he was ready for hopping

Any day now he thought he'd be breathing his last
Any day now his ticker'd stop ticking
He was about to enquire about joining the choir
If he'd a bucket he'd give it a kicking

Life wasn't much cop for poor Eric
What with wheel chairs and zimmers and sticks
And to lighten the load he'd to use a commode
It was starting to get on his wick

He'd a shelf full of pills and an oxygen mask
When he walked he was stooping and hobbling
And next to his knee was a bag for his wee
And his cardy had terminal bobbling

By chance, there was a knock, that night about eight
There was a bloke with a scythe at the door
A salesman no doubt, he says "I'm not selling nowt"
Eric says "Aye, I've heard that one before"

He says "We're doing a survey about croaking,
Have you got any plans for this summer?
I'm sort of enquiring if you've thought of expiring,
Or if you've thought about doing a runner?"

So the bloke shows him a brochure for Heaven
He says "There's not much to do but it's nice,
There's angels and clouds, no noise and no crowds,
And the girls are all sugar and spice"

Eric wasn't convinced he says "You not got owt else?"
Bloke says "Hell's not a bad little spot,
To tell you the truth, it's like Magaluf,
Maybe not quite as noisy and hot"

He says "Some people your age go to Limbo,
It isn't much different to here,
But you cannot join in, cos you're all faded and thin,
And you tend to spill most of your beer"

"You might consider going to Purgatory,
What with you being a Catholic n'that,
But you might get tormented, or end up demented,
And it's a bugger trying to get a flight back"

"If you're looking for summat that's out of this world,
Utopia's supposed to be great,
It's like your best ever dream, all peaches and cream,
Least that's what I've heard, any rate"

Eric says "I don't think much of your options,
In fact bonny lad you can stick it,
It's no bundle of laughter, is this so-called hereafter,
There's no way that I'm buying a ticket"

"I'm better off staying right here where I am,
Despite all me aches and me ills,
I'm feeling all right and there's a match on tonight,
I'll just stay at home, thanks. ....Where's me pills?"

Much Ado About Tadpoles

When I was a lad, I liked lots of pets
Of sticklebacks and newts I was fond
Rabbits cost ower much and you needed a hutch
You'd get tadpoles for nowt at the pond

All you needed to have was an old pair of tights
And you'd cut out the toe with no holes
Then some coat hanger wire bent round with the pliers
And stuffed in the end of a pole

With some string round the neck of a marmalade jar
For to carry them home safe and sound
And a pair of Dad's wellies that came up to me belly
I'd set off to the outskirts of town

Now the smelly pit pond was the best place to go
Over the field at the back of the mission
With some pop and some bait, I'd meet up with me mates
And get down to some serious fishing

So we all waded in, from the shallow bit, like
When it got ower deep we would stop
But I had some bad luck when me welly got stuck
And the water came ower the top

Like I said early on, me Dad's wellies was big
Size twelve and about two foot high
And the fuller they got left me glued to the spot
And only me shoulders were dry

Now you don't need an O-level in Physics to see
That the volume displaced by a boot
Is the height of the side, Pi-R-squared, times how wide
And it works out - two gallons a foot

With eight pints to the gallon I quickly perceived
Getting out wasn't going to be fun
If a pint of cold water weighs a pound and a quarter
Times sixteen...... must be nearly a ton!

Now the problem was noticed by me mate, Bob McGill
His Dad's in the RNLI
So he took control and he reached out a pole
And proceeded to poke out me eye

"Me Dad says don't panic in situations like this"
He screamed at the rest of the lads
He says "Don't stand and stare, send up a flare,
Get the Coastguard, a Fireman .....or me Dad"

So they went for his Dad he was in the top club
He was watching the horses on telly
He arrived in great haste, plodged in up to his waist
And pulled us right out of me wellies

I couldn't care less that I'd only one sock
And me shirt and me strides were all muck
Then I stood on a nettle, tripped over some scrap metal
And rolled in a cowpat for luck

I crept home to the scullery at the back of our house
And I quietly opened the door
But me Mam heard the sneck, grabbed the scruff of me neck
And yelled "Look at the state of me floor"

She got hold of me lug dragged me into the yard
Set about me with an old carpet beater
She says "Wait till your Dad hears you've been a bad lad,
It'll be bed, without watching Blue Peter"

Well, my Dad was going fishing on Sunday that week
That gave me a good seven days spare
To find me a boat or owt that would float
And go and see if his wellies were still there !

Saving For A Rainy Day

They didn't have modern medicine in our day
When you think what doctors can do
Transplantin' folks hearts and other spare parts
And making them feel like brand new

But that wasn't the case with old Eddie
No matter how hard they all tried
Its a pity to say, if he was living today
He'd probably've still been alive

But he'd had his ninety-ninth birthday
So he hadn't done bad, that's the truth
And if he'd just got my mates to fix his loose slates
He would never have slipped off the roof

As usual he'd been trying to save money
But he'd never been short of cash, Eddie
In fact I've heard said, that under his bed
The old bugger had thousands in readies

He was always dead tight with his assets
A miser, and between you and me
You couldn't get him to part wi' the whiff off a fart
He wouldn't give you the steam off his pee

A right niggardly, cheese-paring skinflint
And to save on the funeral expense
He'd even made his own coffin, it cost next to nothing
He'd do owt to save a few pence

He'd have bought second hand if he could have
"Second hand?" says his Jean, he says "Aye"
He checked all around, he says "No more than three pound"
He even looked at the Scouts 'Bring & Buy'

He conceded defeat and he went to his shed
With some boxes and staples and stuff
He hammered and swore for an hour or more
Then he came out looking dead chuffed

It was made out of six cardboard cartons
Stuck together with brown sticky tape
Baked Beans, two Bleaches and two Co-op Peaches
In a rough sort of, coffin type shape

"What's the point of best oak?" he'd once said to his Jean
"It won't have to last long nor nowt,
It would be such a shame, just to go up in flames,
Them Crem lads, they don't muck about!"

"I'll only be going from here to Saint John's,
I'm not the extravagant type,
I'll be nice and snug in that old tartan rug,
Me slippers and a fill for me pipe"

"It won't take much burning, won't cardboard,
And apart from that I'm quite small,
It won't be much fun but they'll soon have me done,
You might get a discount an' all"

The weather had been bad for a couple of weeks
And come the big day it was foggy
When they got down the lane, it started to rain
And the cardboard of the coffin went soggy

Now four pallbearers should've been quite enough
He was only eight stone with a fag
When they got to the door, they needed two more
In the middle, to combat the sag

With his backside sticking out through the bottom
Arms and legs all over the shop
The vicar poor guy just looked to the sky
When a bald head popped out through the top

I mean, Eddie had told him what he wanted to do
And he agreed, mind, he wasn't too keen
There were bits of it dropped all over the shop
Like a Tuesday when the bin man's just been

They scraped up what they could and they made a big pile
Poor Eddie looked owt but serene
He looked owt but snug in a damp tartan rug
"It's his own stupid fault" whispered Jean

It was hardly a dignified send off
A right shambles it was, to be blunt
But she wasn't disheartened by a pile of wet cartons
And poor Eddie in a heap at the front

She says "He got what he paid for, daft bugger,
It's nobody's fault but his own,
If he'd left it to me to pay for the teas,
You'd all have to make your way home"

"But he's been saving up, 'rainy day' and all that,
Well they don't come much wetter than this,
So come on, one and all, to the Plasterer's Hall,
For a nosh up and then we'll get pi......a few sherries eh?"

"I've been in the shoe box he kept under the bed,
And I'm set for life now there's just me,
For all his long life, he gave nowt to his wife,
So I'm going on a bit of a spree"

"You can't take it with you. I'm loaded" shouts Jean
"And poor Eddie's plight is the proof,
I won't have no tears, cos he'd still've been here,
If he'd used it for fixing the roof"

Where Seagulls Dare

Cecil was quite fat for a seagull
On account of him not being fit
He didn't fly much, he was a bit scared of heights
And frightened of water a bit

He used to hitch lifts on the trawlers at Shields
And pinch bits of scraps off the deck
But if he ever got chased and flew off up a height
He turned into a poor nervous wreck

He'd flutter off up to the rigging
And let out a loud seagull cry
He got dizzy and his wings turned to jelly
If ever he had to go high

He was never much cop with the women
The thought of 'em had him scared stiff
He didn't care much for dropping them home
Cos they all lived at the top of the cliffs

These anxieties were doing his head in
He gave up on the trawlers and ships
And hung around the car park at Tynemouth
In the hope of a few fish and chips

But the dietary needs of a seagull
Say nowt about haddock in batter
And with bits of kebabs and cheese pasties
Poor Cecil got fatter and fatter

He'd heard that some seagulls were moving inland
So he thought he might give it a go
And he hitched him a lift on a milkfloat
An electric one that only went slow

He got a ledge on a derelict factory
That suited him down to the ground
And he got himself fit just by flapping about
With all the new friends he had found

He's even found himself a new girlfriend
Built a nest by the factory gates
And his diet's just what the Doctor ordered
He follows the fish van round the housing estates

MR WIFFY

FRESH FISH

If In Doubt, Say Nowt!

There's some folks that's brave and others that's not
If there's danger I'm always quite shy
In fact the scariest thing that I've ever done
Was hold a fence post for a bloke wi' cross eyes

But Charlie the rent man just wouldn't be told
And if he'd just taken heed of advice
He'd not've gone collecting down Store Street
And got scared half to death…..only twice

You see that's where the thugs live, is Store Street
And they've got pit-bulls and rottweilers too
And when they give folks their Giros on Thursdays
Paying their rent's like the last thing they'll do

He was a bit of a sissy was Charlie
Always had been ever since he was young
Softly spoken and drippy wi' specs and buck teeth
And a handshake like a dead bullock's tongue

They said natural causes had caused him to die
Despite the teeth marks in his ankles and knees
The post-mortem said a heart attack most likely
Not helped by falling out of a tree

He was never that well off poor Charlie
So his funeral was a right sad affair
They had a whip round at the Legion for a coffin
And for a vicar to say a few prayers

The vicar said nice things about him
Poor Aggie, his wife was bereft
"When he came into this world he had nothing"
She says "Aye, and he still had most of it left"

I saw Ralphie Clegg, he's just turned 98
He was sitting with Alice Jerome
And she's not much younger, I thought to meself
Not much point in them two going home

Billy Hope down the Legion had put on some grub
Cos funerals always bring on a thirst
But there wouldn't be owt left for us folks had to walk
Cos them what had lifts got there first

But I pushed Ralphie down in his wheel chair
I say 'pushed' but I'd no say in the matter
When we rounded the corner at top of the hill
I held on tight and folks had to scatter

He's game for a laugh is old Ralphie
And he whooped with delight as we sped
Cos he'd a lolly stick in the spokes of his wheelchair
"Sounds like a Norton Commando" he said

Course we got there first, well just after the hearse
Burst through the doors and come to a stop
And we caught Charlie's widow snogging Stan Stokes
He's the undertaker from the Co-op

Now I'm not one to gossip but it's funny, is that
And rumours had always been rife
Charlie was happily married but she wasn't
And course Stan Stokes has just buried his wife

Add to that the fact that Stan lives down Store Street
And he's got two or three big bloody dogs
And here's them two getting amongst it
When both their spouses had just popped their clogs

But I'm saying nowt, I just keep me gob shut
Sometimes it's just best to let be
Like I said at the start there's some folks are brave
And there's others that's not…and that's me!

The Things In Granda's Loft

We had wonderful fun at Brewery Street School
Education was coincidental
The bit that I liked was the playtimes
You'd get out in the yard and go mental

Me and Duffy liked playing Commandoes
All manner of brave escapades
We'd be shooting pretendy machine guns
And chucking pretendy grenades

Miss Simpkins, the one with the nose-hairs
The neck-lump and taxi-door ears
Was on yard duty once when she saw us
And come up with a brilliant idea

Cos that afternoon just before home time
She told the whole class to shut up
She got us all to sit to attention
And she sat there looking dead smug

"We're going to do a project about wartime,
We'll stick lots of things on the walls,
And we'll cut out some bits for a scrap book,
And you can dress up like soldiers and all"

"So tonight" she says "Talk to your parents,
And ask if they've got any things,
From the war that you can borrow to show us,
And we'll discuss whatever you bring"

"But my Dad spent the war in the ship yard"
Said Duffy, in a bit of a state
"It was my dad that built the HMS Hood,
Well actually it was him and his mate"

But Miss Simpkins said that he was still very brave
On account of the air raids and that
And she bet that he still had a gas mask
Even if he never got a tin hat

So we all ran off home dead excited
And as soon as me Dad came from work
I says "Dad, have you got any medals?"
And he just looked and he started to smirk

He says "What would I want with pedals"
I says "Medals, not pedals, man, Dad"
He says "Medals? You'd best ask your Granda,
I'm sure there was one that he had"

I says "What did you do in the war, Dad?"
He says "We need a new screw in the door?"
I says "No, in the WAR, IN THE WAR, Dad"
I says "WHAT DID YOU DO IN THE WAR?"

"Oh, in the war?" he says "I worked down the pit, son,
Cos there would always be coal needing dug,
I couldn't join up for the army,
Cos they reckon I'm deaf in one lug"

"But your Granda's got stuff in the loft, son,
He throws nowt away, the daft bugger"
I says "Can we go after tea, Dad?"
He says "I'd love one, milk and two sugars"

So we went to me Granda's and I told him the score
And as usual the bloke comes up trumps
He says "If you look in the cupboard under the stairs,
There's a couple of old stirrup pumps"

Miss Simpkins was chuffed when she saw what I'd got
And she talked for an hour and a quarter
And she showed us how to put fires out
With a stirrup pump and a bucket of water

So that night I went to me Granda's again
And I told him what the teacher had said
And he said he'd an old ammunition box
With his tools in, out in the shed

So I went and got that and had a quick look around
Found a gas mask still in its case
So he let me take both into school the next day
You should have seen Miss Simpkins's face

She said I was dead good in front of the class
And gave us a sweet from her drawer
So I was straight round me Granda's that night after tea
To see if he had any more

He showed me a photo of his old regiment
He says "There's only three or four left alive"
I says "Look, that's him on the back line, Dad"
And me Dad says "Er, twenty past five"

I said "Have you not got a couple of grenades,
I promise I'd not pull the pin"
He says "Don't be so daft you great ha'porth,
They made us all hand them back in"

He says "Tell you what, in the loft, on the tank,
There's a greatcoat you're welcome to borrow"
I says "Wow, just think of their faces,
If I took that AND your tank in tomorrow"

Go On, Benny. Brag About That!

Benny Suddick fell head first off his roof t'other day
His wife looked and saw him go past
He was shouting out something that had naughty words
That were, it transpired, his last

He'd been up there to sort out the aerial
When his tortoise-shell shoes went and slid
He'd been to the barbers the Tuesday before
If he'd known he'd have saved that three quid

He was never that well liked our Benny
A show off, a bit of a brag
Owt you could do, he could do better
A self-opinionated, jumped up, gas bag

If you bought owt then he'd get one bigger
His antics became quite a farce
If you got a new bike, then he would get two
Mind, you can't ride two bikes wi' one arse

He was a pompous old braggart was Benny
His stories just beggared belief
If you'd been to Tenerife for your holidays
He'd been to Elevenerife

He used to drink every night in the Riveters Arms
So we'd go to the Black Bull instead
Least you'd get to the bar without having to make room
For Benny and his bloody big head

He'd hold court and you just had to listen
To his boastful and brash repartee
And if the topic of conversation ever drifted from him
He'd say "Anyway, lads. Back to me"

He was spinning a line to the barmaid one night
Said he'd a sporty, two-seater, bright red
"I know, man. I've seen it. I saw you drive in,
It's an ex-post office mini-van" she said

The next day he was home watching telly
And the picture, he thought, wasn't too sharp
The last he remembered he was sat on the roof
Then he woke up in a queue for a harp

It would make a change from blowing his own trumpet
He would get the angels all gathered around
And he'd be boastin' he fell over three thousand foot
Before he met up with the ground

His funeral was nowt to write home about
Nowt startlin' for someone's big day
You see Benny's best mates were a bit like his teeth
Few and far between, you could say

But funerals, they still get you thinking
"Be one of us next" said Joe Wood
I says "You'll live for ever you old bugger"
He says "I know! ...and so far so good!"

There was still a good turn-out in spite of all that
I counted about thirty five
In fact, there was folks there that morning
Wouldn't have come if he'd still been alive

At the funeral the vicar spoke fondly
Said "He was modest, unpretentious and kind,
Kept himself to himself and was honest,
'Fact the humblest soul you could find"

Well his Elsie'd never heard so much drivel
And she turned to young Darren, her lad
She says "Go'n have a quick look in that coffin,
Just make double sure it's your dad"

He'd always said that he was going to be buried
On the cliff top at Plodgeborough Head
Aye, it's sad, the poor bugger doesn't know to this day
That she had him cremated instead!

Thank Heaven For Little Gulls

I told you 'bout Cecil the seagull?
Who was frightened of water and heights
Which for a seagull is a bit of a bugger
But somehow he copes with his plight

He doesn't go chasing the trawlers
That would frighten him out of his skin
No, he hangs round the back of the chip shop
And nicks the cods' heads from the bin

He moved inland a while ago - get away from the sea
And he started courting this lass
At this derelict factory at Kenton
And they built a nice nest in the grass

But her folks all lived down at Whitby
And he cringed every time that she'd say
"We'll have to go visit me Mother,
She's got plenty of room, we could stay"

'Cos you see, they live up on the cliff face
And wi' Cecil being that scared of heights
And for him to go there for a weekend
Well that wouldn't be ower bright

What, being perched on a ledge high over the waves?
Soaring about at the end of the pier?
Well he didn't go a bundle on that lark
Just the thought of it made him feel queer

He fretted for weeks did poor Cecil
Then come up with a great compromise
He says "We'll go down to Whitby on Friday"
She says "Ooh what a lovely surprise"

He says "We'll meet up with yer mam down on the beach,
And when you lot bed down for the night,
You go up the cliff wi' yer mother,
And I'll go to the caravan site"

She agreed it was a dead good solution
So she looked up the times of the trains
And they managed to hitch on a guards van
With a canopy to keep off the rain

They met up with her folks on the sea front
And they sat and they had a nice chat
And they had ham and pease pudding sarnies
Off some wife in a 'Kiss-me-quick' hat

Now later, after they'd said their goodnights
Our Cecil set off for his bed
He was just climbing the steps by the bandstand
When he saw this seagull with a bump on his head

"Y'aareet, bonny lad?" says our Cecil
But the seagull just gave a bit squeak
So Cecil put one wing around him
It was then that he noticed his beak

He says "That's an awful long beak for a seagull"
Then he noticed his knobbly knees
He says "Them's awful skinny, them legs you've got there,
Like you need a good feeding to me"

He persevered for a while and stroked the lad's brow
And eventually got him to talk
He says "Give ower calling us a seagull,
I'm a stork, you daft goose, - I'm a stork!"

Then he started to cry, he says "I'm going to get sacked,
'Cos I've got this here parcel, you see,
To be delivered to some lass up in Redcar,
Last Tuesday at quarter to three"

"But I bashed me head on a street light last Monday,
And hurt me wing and me foot the same time,
Don't suppose you could do us a favour?"
Cecil says "Course I can, lad. Any time"

And there, in the corner under a bench
When Cecil had a bit peep
Was a seven pound twelve ounce young lassie
Wrapped up in a nappy asleep

"She's heavier than me" says poor Cecil
As he lifted her up in his beak
He says "Oooh me back" but he managed
But his knees were like starting to creak

So there's a baby in Redcar that was three weeks overdue
On account of a broken-down stork
And a seagull that didn't like flying
And 'course... Redcar's a twenty mile walk!

Amazing Gracie

She was a cantankerous old bugger, Aunt Gracie
Even when she was ninety years old
She would swear black was white, just to get in a fight
Aye, she wasn't the sort to be told

We told her she was too old for a skateboard
We said it would be her downfall
We said "One little slip and you'll need a new hip!"
But you might as well talk to that wall

At the seaside, one day with the bowls club
She was watching some kids in the park
She says to their Flo "I n'arf fancy a go,
It looks easy this skateboarding lark"

Flo says "Don't be so daft, at your time of life?"
It was too late, she'd collared this lad
And while Flo held her sticks, he showed her some tricks
And actually, she wasn't too bad

She zig-zagged round the lake a couple of times
And with each lap she got bolder and bolder
She found she went quicker with her skirt in her knickers
And her handbag slung over her shoulder

Now if she'd called it a day, that would've been that
But she had to show off to her mates
She gave us a scare when she flew in the air
And disappeared out through the gates

Well the park's at the top of Plodgeborough Hill
And that would've stopped you or me
But ninety or not, she was away like a shot
Past the arcades and down to the sea

She hit a puddle on the road by the sea front
And her specs got all covered in muck
I would swear to this day, that she had right-of-way
But the other bloke had the big truck

She bounced off the bonnet, up over the rails
She lost her hat and her specs and her fag
She cleared the cliff face and sank without trace
Cos she still had her bowls in her bag

Her Walter was out clipping the privet
When the Panda pulled up at the door
When he saw the Cop's face he knew it was Grace
She'd been arrested quite often before

He says "What's she done this time then? Fighting?"
He says "No, it's more serious than that,
Her and her antics, everyone's frantic,
She's gone into the sea, the daft bat!"

"She's got the Air-Sea Rescue all working flat out,
And the lifeboat checking out round the cliffs,
There's a diver gone down, just to see if she's drowned,
And he came up with a few of her bits"

He showed Walter some stuff in a polythene bag
Walter says "Aye, right enough, it's all hers"
There was a pack of Beechnut and her old rabbit's foot
And the Saint Christopher she kept in her purse

But after three days they gave up on the search
And Walter came to terms with his loss
He says "If she's lost at sea, that's all right by me,
Least I'll save on the funeral costs"

Now a few months had passed and the phone rings
Voice says "That you, Walter?" Walter says "Aye"
"This is the Coastguard, I'm down at the boatyard,
Your Grace's been washed up nearby"

"You're joking" says Walter "Are you sure it's our Grace?
It's nigh on six months she's been gone"
He says "Aye, it's your lass, cos we found her bus pass,
And she's still got her elbow pads on"

"But mind" says the Coastguard, "She doesn't look grand,
Not a pretty sight, a bit bashed
Her perm's a right mess and there's holes in her dress,
And there's two great big lobsters attached"

"What d'you want done?" says the Coastguard
"We'll have to get the poor soul out of sight"
Walt says "I'll pop down the beach, have one lobster each,
And we'll set her again for tonight!"

The Night We Comforted Algernon Pratt

In Plodgeborough, next to the dog track
There's a street leading up from the shop
Two rows of back to back houses
With the big council tip at the top

Now the house at the end that was nearest the tip
Belonged to Algernon Pratt
It was dead handy for odd bits of carpet
And even better if you didn't mind rats

I was just passing, on me way for some oil cloth
To nail on the roof of me shed
When the ambulance delivered old Algie
With bandages from his toes to his head

He had tubes, he had pipes, he had wiring
Sticking in him and some coming out
He could hardly talk, he was in a bad way
So I gave his wife Bessie a shout

"Wotcheor, Mrs Pratt, he's a bit of a state,
What the hell's he been up to this time?"
She says "Daft bugger's been ski-ing in Norway"
And Algie just gave a bit whine

But it wasn't the ski-ing that did it
He had the flu and the cold made it worse
He'd sneezed and he fell off the chairlift
And landed, well ......everything first!

"There's nowt more they can do now" says Bessie
"He's a fair age you know, ninety one,
So I thought he'd be best in his own bed"
Then she whispered "He hasn't got long"

I says "That's terrible news, what with the Leek Show,
But don't forget if there's owt I can do,
She says "As a matter of fact if you're doing nowt,
I've got a hairdressers' appointment at two"

"If you wouldn't mind keeping him company,
Just in case there's owt that he needs"
I said "I'd be delighted" and sat meself down
It's nice when you can do a good deed

So I sat and with a struggle we got talking
He passed me some grapes and he coughed
"You can have them Brazil nuts, they're no use to me,
Not once the chocolate's sucked off"

Well we sat and we talked and we shared a few jokes
And I think that I fair cheered him up
So I said that I'd bring up the lads from the pub
And we'd get a few cans in to sup

So after the Leek Show that Saturday
We settled down for a decent night's drink
Then the conversation got round to old Algie
"Should we go up and see him, do you think?"

Joe says "He'd be delighted to see us,
All his old pals from the snug"
"There's no time like the present" says Archie
"Why don't we go now then?" says Doug

"Cos there's still a good three hours drinking"
Says Cliffy, giving him a clout
Then Robbo says "Aye, but we'll take a few cans,
And we'll take Algie a bottle of stout"

"We'll just have another swift pint for the road"
Says Cliffy, getting them in
"I'll have a quick nip around with the domino" says George
"And we'll take Bessie a bottle of gin"

"She drinks Cherry-B's, man" says Cliffy
"The lasses here all drink the same"
"So which one's Algie, again?" says Walter
He's never been that good with names

So there was just the fifteen of us set off up the hill
And hey, it's a fair bloody march
So when we got up to the Riveters Arms
Cliffy says "We'll stop for a pint, eh? I'm parched"

Davy hit a winning streak on the bandit
So instead of having one, we had three
And by the time we got up past the Buffs Club
We all had to pop in for a wee

Now they don't like you just using their toilets
You know what the club's like for rules
So we all had to have a quick pint in the bar
Then Cliffy went and fell off a stool

So we got him a medicinal brandy
Just to steady his nerves, sort of style
Fred says "I might as well get a round in,
Cos it looks like we'll be here a while"

It takes such a time to pull fifteen pints
There was some of us had time for two
And by then you're needing the toilet again
And by this time there's a bit of a queue

But anyway, we supped up and we went on our way
But by now it had started to rain
So we nipped into the Tavern, just to keep dry
Cliffy says "God, is it my round again?"

We were a bit piddly paddly when we got to the house
I says "Sssh, show a bit of respect"
But Bessie was right pleased to see us
She says "It'll be your last chance, I expect"

"He shouldn't be drinking with the way that he's held"
But Cliffy says "We'll help him out"
Alfie says "I'd lay down me life for me country,
But there's no way I'd ever drink stout"

In an effort not to show our emotions
We acted like nowt was the matter
Cliffy says "What you doing in bed you lazy old sod,
Get up and we'll have a bit natter"

Alfie says "What's going on here, skiving again?
There's no need to take to your bed,
If you'd wanted to get out of the gardening,
Or the housework, you should've just said"

"Taking folks grapes is a bit of a con,
False pretences and that" says Big Ray
"We've put your name down as goalie for Thursday,
So you'd better be feeling okay"

We were doing a good job, we told a few jokes
And in spite of the pain he was in
We took his mind off things, like a diversion
And his bandages managed to grin

Then Bessie says "Would you lads like a sandwich?
Cheese and pickle, to go with your beer?"
She says "I'm saving the ham for the funeral"
I says "Sssh, keep your voice down, he'll hear"

But we needn't have bothered being subtle
Cos big Ray who'd had far too much beer
Bashed his head on the way to the lav and he swore
"God! - We'll not get the coffin through here!"

Bravetart

Tessa and Jill were at a do 'bove the Co-op
They spent all night just watching the door
They were eyeing up folks and making sly jokes
'Bout their hair-dos and the clothes what they wore

Then Tessa says "Jill" She says "What?" She says "Look"
She says "Where?" She says "There, at that Val,
That top's not just strapless, it's see-through and backless"
Jill says "Eeh, Tess, shut up. She's your pal"

Tessa says "Aye, I know that. I know she's a mate,
But if there's one thing that gets on me nerves,
It's dressing up like a fifteen quid salad,
And showing off all of her curves"

Jill says "You're right and you know, I'm not one to talk,
But have you seen the length of that skirt,
And those wobbly heels do owt but appeal,
And just look at the way that she flirts"

"Look at her slobbering over poor Davy Dobson,
She'll be wanting to drag him backstage,
She's not going to be long in that top she's got on,
And she's revealing everything but her age"

"She heard that he likes women wi' dimples,
So she's been stood there giving him the eye,
I think it's quite simple, he'll go right off dimples,
When he sees the state of her thighs"

"And look at the way that she's dancing about,
You'd think she was just a bit kid"
"How old is she then?" "She'll not see forty again"
"She wouldn't recognise it if she flamin' well did"

"Just who the hell does she think that she is?
Don't she know she's not facially gifted"
"She's ugly, you mean. The word's there to be used,
It's about time she had that face lifted"

"And look at the state of that lipstick she's on,
She's got it all over her fag,
She's got a bum like a Cullercoats donkey,
She's like Bernard Bresslaw in drag"

"That's no disrespect to poor Mister Bresslaw,
But she's waddling about like a hen,
And that frock that she's wearin's in danger of tearin',
She's been poured in and forgot to say when"

"Her thighs" Tessa says "They're like lumpy blancmange,
And her calves like the underground map,
And look at her chin" "You mean chins" says our Jill
"Like four piglets caught in a trap"

"She's got boobs like a dead heat in a zeppelin race,
When she turns round you see folks dive for cover,
And that new Wonderbra, now that's takin' it too far,
It's a wonder she doesn't fall over"

"She says she's not fat and she fits a fourteen,
But I think she's been fibbing a bit"
Jill says "I don't believe that, cos if she isn't fat,
Then her skin's not a very good fit"

"Mind I saw her last week and she really likes you"
"She speaks well of you too" says our Tessa
She says "Don't get me wrong, I know she's headstrong,
But I'll have nowt said against the lass, bless her"

Hey There, Geordie Gull!

There's a seagull called Cecil on Tyneside
I'm sure you've all probably heard
That he's not keen on heights and hates flying
It's a bugger, is that, for a bird

He walks everywhere, does Cecil the seagull
Or he hitches a lift when he can
On a train or a wagon or summat
But mostly on Joe's ice cream van

It's a funny old van, Joe Quadrini's
A pretend spaceship sits on the roof
Which for Cecil is quite warm and quite comfy
'Fact it's luxury, tell you the truth

In the summer Joe goes down the seafront
So Cecil tags along for the ride
And the kids look out for the ice cream man
And the spaceship with a seagull inside

One day at the visitors' centre
Cecil was raking round bins for some scraps
When he noticed a concerned looking pigeon
Who was looking for summat on the map

"Y'aareet mate?" say's Cecil, "You lost then?
Are you needing a hand? What's the crack?"
The pigeon says "Je m'appele Pierre, I'm from Paris,
Je suis buggered if I can find me way back"

"I 'ave no sense, 'ow you say, of direction,
Je suis crap at zis 'oming malarkey,
But they keep shipping me off to some far away place,
And your climate I find a tad parky"

"Aye, it's not ower hot" says our Cecil
Sort of putting Pierre at his ease
"But divvent ye worry, wus'll soon get yer hyem"
But Pierre he says "Speak English please"

So Cecil spoke louder and slower
And suggested he'd best go by air
He says "You'd best get a plane from the airport"
Pierre says "How ze hell will I find me way there"

"Nowt's the bother, bonny lad," says our Cecil
Raising his voice to a shout
"You can come for a ride in me spaceship,
And we'll get you to the airport for nowt"

The pigeon stood open mouthed when he saw it
"Zut alors, zis is, ow-you-say, trendy?"
But Cecil says "Divvent get carried away,
It's not real, you know, it's only pretendy"

Joe Quadrini had just sold his last ninety-nine
And was shutting up shop to go home
When the pigeon and the seagull hopped onto his roof
So he chucked them a few broken cones

Then he drove them away on the Old Coast Road
But then started to swear and to shout
All the traffic was bumper to bumper
Cos the Ministry was just getting out

They were stuck outside Four Lane Ends Metro
When Cecil grabbed hold of Pierre
He says "Howway, bonny lad, sod this for a lark,
We'll hop on that tram ower there"

They hopped on just in time as the tram pulled away
And the ride from then on was quite rough
And they had to hang on to the buffers
Cos the roof's all electrics and stuff

But it only took twenty two minutes
They'd to change at South Gosforth of course
And by the time that they got to the airport
They both felt they'd been kicked by a horse

But they soon found a trolley full of cases
'Charles De Gaulle Airport' it read
Cecil shouts "Hop on and mind, keep yer heed doon"
Pierre says "Je ne comprehend pas what you said"

"Orry vwa then," says Cecil, "Hope you get home okay,
And divvent eat ower many croissants"
But Pierre just looked at him like was daft
So he looked at him back, like he wasn't

He could see the poor pigeon was frightened
But doing his best to be brave
Then a truck come and pulled at the trolley
And he sobbed and gave Cecil a wave

And when Cecil got home and settled down for the night
He was starting to have a few doubts
About Pierre stuck at Charles De Gaulle airport
And still trying to find the way out!

The Great Amblethwaite Cap Mystery

He was a right flamin' fidget was Alec McGarr
And one night, his best mate Jimmy Gower
Says "For heavens sake Mac, what you doing with your cap?
You've been fiddling best part of an hour"

He says "Summat's not right, see it got wet last night,
So it got hung on the fender to dry,
I must've been drunk, you see the caps gone and shrunk,
But the linings sort of stayed the right size"

"Time you'd a fresh'n, you've had that since the depression,
I can remember it once had a pattern,
It don't owe you nowt, why don't you splash out?
Get a new'n and chuck away that'n"

Mac says "You needn't talk, yours is old as the hills,
I'll only get one if you do an' all"
Jimmy thought for a mo then said "Okay then, right-o,
There's a cap shop next door to the Town Hall"

So the very next day they checked the display
In the window before they went in
There was felts there was tweeds 'fact owt you might need
And yet Mac chose the same one as Jim

"That's not a problem," said the man serving on
"They come in all sizes and shapes,
Even blue ones and reds, now give us your heads"
Then he measured them both with a tape

"Right, seven and three quarters, that's the one that fits you,
And yours sir, is five and seven eighths"
Mac turned round and said "You've got a big head!"
Jim says "What's two flamin' inch between mates?"

The man showed them the caps, best Donegal Tweed
And they tried 'em and they fitted dead good
Then he wrapped them in two brown paper parcels
And they paid him and left. Like you would

Mac says "I'm excited" Jim says "I'm delighted"
So they nipped into the Swan for a dram
It was three hours later they fell out of the pub
With their parcels and went for the tram

They carried their packages up on the top deck
And sat in two seats at the back
"Can't wait till the chaps see our spanking new caps"
"Hic, and so's I an' all too" said Mac

But that night when they met in the Plasterers Arms
There was neither of em wearing their hats
Mac says "Mine's the wrong size, it fell down over me eyes"
Jim says "That's a coincidence, that"

"Cos mine's far to small it was no use at all,
Sat on top of me head like a bap,
I'm going back and play hell" "Aye, and I am as well,
He'll get the sharp end of me tongue'll that chap"

So they met the next day outside of the shop
"You know, I'm not really a complainer" said Jim
"No, I'm not an'all - and that bloke's really tall"
So they went into the Swan for two gins

They'd a couple of quick'uns then a couple more slow
Washed down with a couple of stouts
Then a couple of beers just to keep their heads clear
Then they picked up their parcels and went out

They got to the cap shop, Mac pushed Jim in first
"I've a complaint!" "You've a what?" said the bloke
"A complaint" He says "Oh?" Jim said "Aye" He says "So?"
"It's these caps. Were you having a joke?"

"A joke?" said the bloke "I don't do that to folk"
"Well how d'you explain this then" Mac said
And he took out his cap from the brown paper wrap
And plonked it on top of his head

Then says "Heavens above… bugger fits like a glove,
That's funny cos it didn't last night"
So Mac tried his on and it fit, whereupon
They both turned as red as back lights

They apologised and left with their tails 'tween their legs
"Summat strange happened there, don't you think?"
Said Mac, scratching his head "I'm quite puzzled" Jim said
So they popped into the Swan for a drink

Now as true as I'm standing here telling this tale
You'll not guess what happened that night
After Jim had his nap he went to put on his cap
And blow me but the bugger was tight

And Mac, at his place, had just washed his face
And went to put on his cap to go out
But instead of being snug it fell down over his lugs
"What the bloody hell's going on here?" he shouts

So they're still wearing their old caps are poor Jim and Mac
The strange phenomenon was never resolved
They've a theory or two, 'spect you've got one too
They think a sinister force was involved

And from that day on, they've never drunk in the Swan
They don't trust the landlord it's said
They think it's quite clear, he puts stuff in his beer
That alters the size of folks' heads

Don't Go Changing

Last April, Ruby Ruddick, down Bolsover Street
Was out giving her step a good scrubbing
Whilst Leonard, her lodger, was in the netty out back
Giving his boots a good claggin' wi' dubbin

Ruby shouted 'Good morning' to the folks walking past
Didn't have to look up, knew their boots
But the morning in question, she saw a posh pair of brogues
Attached to some legs in a suit

And there stood this bloke, fancy tie, bowler hat
"I'm from London" he says, she says "So?
That's not my fault, are you wanting a medal?"
He says "I'm from Littlewoods Pools." She says "Oh"

He says "Besides, it's not you, it's your lodger I want"
"Just my luck" says poor Rube "You might know"
She dropped her brush in her bucket and got up off her knees
She says "Come through then." He says "Oh, right-o"

He followed her in down the lobby and through to the back
"Who is it? Sod off!" shouts the budgie
She showed him through the back scullery and into the yard
And she knocked on the door of the cludgie

Leonard shouts "Are you bustin? Just give us a mo"
But the bloke just says "No take your time,
You've won half a million on Littlewoods' Pools,
You've got eight score draws on one line"

Well Lenny jumped up, he thought "What?" he says "Eh?"
I don't think he quite understood fully
All exuberant like, banged his head on the bike
That was hanging in there on a pulley

He opened the door, had a look at the cheque
And started to do a bit dance
The bloke says "I'll shake hands when you've washed 'em,
But first you'd best pull up your pants"

"Said nowt about this in his horoscope last night"
Said Ruby feeling quite faint
But being a regular churchgoer
She said "Thank you, oh Lord. You're a saint"

He decided to live life like he'd not done before
On account of he'd never had funding
With a spare collar and pants in his old haversack
He set off on the train down to London

The first thing he noticed when he got to Kings Cross
Was all the well dressed looking fellers
"That's the new me" he thought and went out and bought
A new suit, bowler hat and umbrella

He blew seven and six in the Dicken's Tea Rooms
Pot of tea and two sausage rolls
Then he went for a haircut at a barber's, so posh
It didn't have a red and white pole

"Would sir like a nice cut and a blow dry?"
Said the toffee-nosed barber quite smugly
He says "Go on then son, but d'you think while you're on
You can do owt about us being so ugly?"

"Well actually" says the bloke "There's a clinic upstairs,
Does facelifts and things while-you-wait,
They could reshape your nose and straighten that chin"
And Leonard thought "That would be great"

He got his hair done all nice then he toddled upstairs
And a bloke helped him pick a new nose
Then he put him to sleep and fitted it on
Along with two lugs what he'd chose

So Leonard took lodgings for a couple of days
And by the third day, right enough, looked just super
It was better by far, like a real film star
In fact he looked just like what's-his-name Cooper

Now the next thing he wanted was a nice shiny car
To impress Ruby and all of their mates
So he went into a showroom and slapped down the cash
For a brand spanking Ford Anglia estate

He drove back to Ruby's she was there at the step
Faffin' on like an old mother hen
And his horoscope had said summat about church bells
So he proposed to her right there and then

She was all overcome when he got down on one knee
Cos the step was still wet, like as not
"You don't look too good but you do a canny leek pud,
Should we go and get wed then, or what?"

She'd never seen him behave so romantic before
But she agreed and said "Aye, might as well"
So they drove round to speak to the Minister
Who was up a height fixing one of his bells

He looked down and shouts "Aalreet, Pet" to Ruby
But as he did he let go of the rope
And a two ton bell landed on Leonard
Which just shows you can't trust horoscopes

When Leonard woke up he saw Pearly Gates
You can imagine he was feeling quite sick
And Ruby went spare that night saying prayers
She says "God, that was a right dirty trick"

As usual, not expecting an answer from God
She nearly dropped dead when he spoke
He says "What's the to-do, was it someone you knew?"
She says "Aye, it was Leonard. Me bloke"

He says "Len?" She says "Aye" "In a suit and a tie?
It didn't look nowt like him" said God
"All them fancy new clothes, new lugs and new nose,
I didn't know it was him, the daft sod!"

The Graveyard Shift

There's nowt ever happens in our neck of the woods
That's Plodgeborough, up north, where it's cold
The death rate's pretty normal, that's one thing
It's about one death per person, I'm told

Now you know that I'm not one to gossip nor nowt
But I thought you should know all the same
You know Freddie Norris? Well when he passed away
There's not one person said "That's a shame"

One thing folks can't stand is a moaner
And a right grouchy old whiner was Fred
He wouldn't spare feelings if owt was amiss
He'd say the first thing that come into his head

And just to be awkward he picked winter
The ground was as hard as bell metal
The plot was the far end of the graveyard
And surrounded with brambles and nettles

"He just did that on purpose," said old Geordie Nick
Whose job it was to dig graves
"Decent folks would've waited till springtime,
It'll take a good two or three days"

Poor lad chiselled and dug with a pick and a spade
From seven o'clock Thursday morn
And by nightfall on Friday he was just about done
"I think I'll off home now" he yawned

He was too tired to bother with covers or owt
He just wheeled all his stuff to his shed
Locked up his steps and his shovels and things
And wandered off home to his bed

There's always been a shortcut through the graveyard
Through the hedge and then down over the stile
Cos if you had to walk round then back up the hill
Must be getting on for a mile

So there's Cliffy on his way from the Riveters Arms
Friday night after spending his dole
Come staggering through the gap in the privet
Tripped up and went straight down the hole

He was dazed for a while then he slowly came round
And he cursed when he saw there's no ladder
It was half an hour or more since he'd come out the pub
And he was needing to empty his bladder

So he was resigned to the fact that it would be quite a while
And he pulled up his collar and sat
He wrapped himself up in that day's Racing Post
And thought to himself "Well, that's that"

"There's no use complaining" thought Cliffy
As he lay in the dark undeterred
"I've seen lads in the war got their heads blown off,
And you never heard them say a word"

He managed to sleep for an hour quite soundly
He'd spent worse nights at El Alamein
The effects of the brandy came in quite handy
Cos he was certainly feeling no pain

Now all this time, close by, just over the hedge
In the shelter by the thirty-nine stop
Young Darren McGuire had been having a snog
With Nell Hutton from Wilkinson's shop

He put her on the last bus and climbed through the hedge
And he turned to give her a wave
Got his foot caught up in the brambles
And went flying head first in the grave

He panicked a bit, poor lad, well you would
And he clawed at the sides to get out
He jumped up and down like something not right
And then he started to scream and to shout

"You've no chance," said Cliffy, "I've been trying meself,
You might as well come here and sit"
And you know, though it was steep he got out in one leap
Hearing a voice in the dark helped a bit!

He never turned round he just ran and he ran
With all manner of grizzly thoughts
"That's the last time that I take a shortcut through there,
And that's the last time I'll ever drink shorts"

"There was no need for that," thought poor Cliffy
"Must've been summat I said"
And he curled up again with his Racing Post
And pulled his jacket up ower his head

He kipped for an hour, it could've been more
Then he woke but it still wasn't day
And he thought he could hear someone singing
And he knew by the song it was Ray

"Irene, goodnight Irene"
He was singing at the top of his voice
He'd blown all his cash at a lock-in
So he had to walk home, he'd no choice

"Champion," says Cliffy, "That's my mate, Big Ray"
They were best mates mind, almost like brothers
But when Cliffy shouts "Giz a hand, pal. I'm freezing"
Ray says "You shouldn't have kicked off your covers"

And with that he staggered off, started singing again
Oblivious to poor Cliffy's plight
With three steps forward and two and a half back
Getting home was going to take him all night

When Geordie Nick turned up the next morning
Poor Cliffy was turning quite blue
Geordie sees him and shouts "Hey, move over,
There's needier cases than you"

He passed down the ladder and reached out a hand
Poor Cliffy could only just speak
He says "I know I've only been here eight hours,
But I feel like I've been here three weeks"

"That's as near to dying as I'd like to get"
Says Cliffy as he started to climb
"I know that you only die once in your life,
But it must last an awful long time!"

The Fire in Nan's Front Room

There was a whiff of bad eggs when Nan came in the room
"Is that you, Fred?" she says "What's that stink?"
And Fred, who'd been sat fast asleep in his chair
Says "It's that gas fire. It's gone on the blink"

She says "Right. You'll have to wait for your dinner,
That fire's never been nowt but trouble"
She says "I'm going to that Gas Board to play merry hell"
And she set off down the town at the double

She marched down the High street like a woman possessed
She was focussed like a Grand National winner
Apart from calling at the Pork shop on the High Street
To pick up some pies for their dinner

Now folks round our way are scared of Nan Burke
And at the Gas Board she caused quite a din
The staff were aware they'd best treat her with care
In the frame of mind like what she was in

She banged down her pies on the counter
So as not to leave no one in doubt
And in a voice that she kept for occasions like such
"I want someone important" she shouts

The Acting Deputy Chargehand was called for
A young lad wi' spots and fair hair
But his knees started itching and his backside was twitching
When he saw it was Nan Burke standing there

He politely directs her to a blue telephone
Even though she had give him the jitters
He says "Lift up the handset and press number nine,
And they'll put you straight through to the fitters"

Now being impatient, and her pies getting cold
And nowt happening the first couple of times
Gave the Acting Deputy Chargehand one of her looks
And continued to press number nine

Now having dialled nine, nine, nine, a voice t'other end
Said "Emergency - which service d'you require?
"It's a fire," says our Nan, "Can you send round a man?"
The voice says "Aye, right away. Where's the fire?"

"It's in me front room" says our Nan, quite abrupt
And they asked her to give her address
Then they asked if there's anyone still in the house
She says "Aye, and he's not even dressed"

They said they'd get someone around straight away
And Nan said "Okay, fair enough"
Then she thought "Just a tick, I'd best get home quick"
Cos Fred's hearing aid battery was duff

He wasn't daft, wasn't Fred, well he was, but not much
And he'd turned off the gas at the meter
And he'd opened the living room windows
And looked out the old paraffin heater

He'd got it going and was dead nice and cosy
With his feet up just warming his toes
When a dirty great axe came through the front door
Followed by five great big blokes with a hose

Then another climbed in through the window
With an oxygen mask, helmet and wellies
And chucked Fred across his left shoulder
And sent his teeth flying down back of the telly

Then they filled Nan's front room full of water and foam
And created a right ballyhoo
You see the firemen in Amblethwaite don't get many fires
So they make the most of the ones that they do

Now the Fire Chief, the one in the white helmet
Arrived and had a quick look about
And declared if indeed that there had been a fire
It was now well and truly put out

When he saw water pouring out of the letterbox
He complimented his men on their work
And decided they'd best do a runner
When he realised that the house was Nan Burke's

Poor Fred was just dumped in the garden
In jama bottoms and string vest he was stood
And when Nan found out he would get a good clout
So he legged it up Amblethwaite woods

He's been up there a month now he daresn't come home
Well not until the parlour dries out
He's found an old hut, lives on berries and nuts
All the stuff that he learned in the Scouts

That Acting Deputy Chargehand from the Gas Board
He's done a bunk an' all, it's reported
And if he's got any sense, he'll learn self-defence
Cos Nan's gas fire's still not been sorted!

The Wild Look In Gladys' Eyes

*(This one was written with the help of Bernard Wrigley
and Oldham's number one monologuist Stan Brown)*

On Saturdays, there's a do 'bove the Co-op
It costs one-and-six to get in
Round our way they call it 'The Social'
It's run by Jessop, a bloke wi' no chin

His wife brings a teapot for folks that like tea
And for young 'uns she sells pop and crisps
And for them that gets peckish wi' dancing
She's got Mars bars and a few walnut whips

With his gramophone and big box of records
He sits there all pompous and that
He's a bit of a toff, Mister Jessop
You know the sort - wears a cravat

He plays waltzes and military two-steps
Bradford Barn, Gay Gordons and such
I don't think he's ever heard of The Tremeloes
In fact he's a bit out of touch

But the young 'uns don't go for the dancing
Lads and lasses all go there to score
And to neck-on for three or four hours
And drink cider from the Offy next door

Now Waggitshaw's lass was there, Gladys
Forty six, just approaching her prime
Six foot three, nineteen stone of pure woman
She could carry me to me bath any time

She was good in a fight, was young Gladys
The sort who'd be best as your mate
And though most of the time she's a softie
You wouldn't pinch a spud off her plate

But her choice of men left you frustrated
Like Tadger the trucker from Teams
Or Percy the pig man from Pegswood
All tow-rags if you know what I mean

Gladys went out the back to the toilets
Where couples were having a snog
And she noticed these two getting amongst it
When she looked under the door of the bog

As soon as she saw who the bloke was
She was stunned - nearly let go her beer
It was Percy the pig man from Pegswood
Nibbling chunks from some hussy's left ear

This didn't seem right to our Gladys
Though he stunk a bit, Percy was hers
So she pulled him away from the floozie
And knocked him down two flights of stairs

Gladys wasn't content with just Percy
She punched three of his mates' heads as well
Her face it was turning quite purple
Mr Jessop looked and thought 'Bloody Hell'

He peeked down the stairs and saw Percy
Then the strange look in Gladys' eyes
Poor Jessop went faint and his legs sort of went
As she picked up her bag and let fly

There followed a strange situation
Where aristocratic types win
Being struck by some angry bint's handbag
Doesn't hurt if you haven't a chin

This person-powered paisley projectile
Sailed straight underneath Jessop's lips
Hit the wall at the side and exploded
In a sea of Mars bars and Smiths crisps

The floozie knew when she wasn't quite wanted
She'd been there a few times before
She decided she'd best make an exit
And limbo'd out under the door

Old Jessop wasn't hurt he'd just fainted
And was lying there flat on his back
As Gladys scooped all the crisps in her handbag
Or else there'd be no midnight snack

Then her maternal side kind of took over
It just sort of rushed to the fore
When she looked at the state of poor Jessop
Laying pole-axed and limp on the floor

"The Kiss of Life" she shouts, laying the lips on
In one mad and passionate crush
Now Jessop's ditched his wife for our Gladys
And the two of 'em live over the brush

Jessop's dull life is now changed for ever
He's now wearing wide kipper ties
And pants that are flared at the bottom
And sunglasses even when it's not bright

They still have the do 'bove the Co-op
Each Saturday night like before
But Jessop's now billed as the DeeJay
And Gladys is in charge of the door

Now no-one pokes fun at our Gladys
Or laughs at Jessop and his bold choice of ties
They remember that do at the Social
And the wild look in Gladys' eyes

The Answer Lies In The Soil

You know the private houses up by the Library?
The 'Lace-curtains-and-kippers' estate?
There's some's got bay windows wi' lead on
And there's some folks got wrought iron gates

There's some got high fences wi' Keep Out written on
And stone lions either side of the path
There's some's got fur coats and no knickers
But we'd better not get into that

Well Abraham Gow from the book shop
No family, just lives on his own
He's the house with the massive big garden
Monkey-puzzle tree and six gnomes

And mind, he keeps it all lovely
He's got a lawn that's all stripey and flat
A nice tidy hedge runs right round it
He's got hydrangeas and hostas n'that

Now there's me I haven't got a big garden
The wife tire's too easy you see
I've even had the coal bunker brought close to the door
She's bone idle if you ask me

But we've always a nice show of roses
We've won first prize at the flower show twice
They take a bit pampering and coaxing
But they always come out looking nice

Now I was out doing some pruning last Easter
And there's Abraham comes walking past
He just took one look at me roses
And he held on to the wall and he gasped

Well I thought he was having a one of his turns
I got quite a shock, the daft bat!
"I say, my good man, they're terrific"
He says "How on earth does one grow them like that"

He talks a bit posh does old Abey
In his tweeds you would think he's the squire
But he's holes in his shoes and his elbows
Born a gentleman but never required

He says "You'll have to let me in on your secret, old chap,
Does one spray them with something obscure?"
He says "Mine are all puny and listless"
I says "Your soil man. You need some manure"

So I popped past that Sunday, he was ironing his lawn
I saw his roses and had a bit look
I says "It's as plain as the nose on your face, man
They need a good claggin wi' muck"

"Fertiliser, you mean?" he says in his posh voice
Like he's got a pound note for a tongue
I says "You can call it whatever you like, mate"
I says "Dung man, you need a bit dung"

"Where on earth does one go to get something like that?"
I could see that he wasn't too keen
I says "You'll have to go ower yon top side,
There's a farmer up there, name of Green"

"He's the best bloke around here for that stuff" I says
"He sells bags of it all the year round,
And if you ask him he'll even deliver,
You get a wagon load for just a few pounds"

So that weekend he set off ower yon top side
He had to borrow a bike from his mate
There wasn't much chance he could miss it
He just followed his nose to the gate

In fact his nose stuck up more than it usually did
As he tried not to sniff too much air
And he found Farmer Green in the pig pen
He approached him as near as he dared

He says "Now then young man, I'm told you can help"
And he squelched as he stepped off his bike
"I'm told your manure is second to none"
The farmer says "Aye. What sort would you like?"

He says "Oh, there's a choice? How foolish of me,
I'm sorry, I'm not really sure"
Farmer Green says "Well that's not a problem,
Come on and I'll give you a tour"

He says "Now this one's the very best pig muck"
Then he took him round the back of the barn
He says "If it's well rotted cow dung you're after,
Use this and you'll come to no harm"

If it's roses you might try our horse muck,
It's the best that you'll get in these parts,
Or there's sheep dung, hand picked by the missus,
That'll make your roses look smart"

He had bags of the stuff all with labels
Poor Abe had never smelt such a pong
There was hens, there was goats there was allsorts
Then Abraham says "Er, don't get me wrong…,"

"But I need to be sure it's good quality"
He sounded a right townie twit
And the farmer just looked at him disgusted
He says "Hey lad, we don't sell no shit!"

Cissie Stobbs and the Census Man

Plodgeborough, you know, is quite picturesque
But there's an eyesore on the outskirts of town
They built three multi-storeys where the woods used to be
And named the flats after the trees they chopped down

Now at number twenty seven 'The Conkers'
Lives a lass that's the talk of the bread van
No stranger to blokes and the bottle
And a pain in the neck for the rent man

I expect you'll have heard of young Cissie Stobbs
There's not many round here who'll have not
She's got two flats together in The Conkers
To make room for the kids what she's got

That's right she's got twelve, or she had the last count
But there's never no bloke on the scene
Well there is now and then but they don't hang about
More'n an hour, if you know what I mean

Aye, she never went short of a feller or three
She'd that many she used to lose track
She was a bit of a glamour puss, Cissie
She had blonde hair but now it's gone black

One day in the park the Parkie had said
"Is this a picnic or a kiddies day out?"
Poor Peg gave a whine, she says "No, they're all mine,
It's no picnic, I'll tell you for nowt"

Then she sussed out what was causing the babies
And a boatload of Mothers-in-Law
Now thinks kids, specially lads, should be seen and not had
She's not on squeaking terms with her bed any more

But she's a good Mum is Cissie. Puts the kids first
Makes sure that they don't go without
And she puts up wi' the jokes about all of them blokes
Who had her when she knew nowt

The middle one, Wayne, once said "Mother?
Did my dad have red hair like mine?"
So she thought for a mo and said "I don't really know,
He was wearing a cap at the time"

Now Wayne's little brother was listening in
It's strange but he's called Wayne too
In fact all twelve's the same, they all answer to Wayne
'Cept their Susan who answers to 'Sue'

"Was he my Dad as well, this bloke wi' the cap?"
Said the other Wayne, sat on her knee
"No, your dad was the boss at the Odeon,
He used to get us in the posh seats for free"

Then Skinny Wayne said "Well, what I'd like to know,
Is how come our Wayne here's so fat?"
"His dad was a butcher, there was a war on, you know,
I'd to think about me rations and that"

Then Wayne, the third youngest, he pipes up an all
Cos he'd been pretty quiet throughout
He says "My dad musn't've been very big then,
So is that why I'm just three foot nowt?"

"That's cos you're five, you daft bugger" says Ma
"Your dad was a good six foot three,
You'll end up dead tall like our Wayne here,
Just wait till you're big and you'll see"

So then Wayne butted in, he's the eldest but one
"What was my father like, then?" he asks
She says "I'm not sure, there was an air-raid gan' on,
And we all had to wear our gas masks"

She was grateful that the eldest wasn't in on the game
Cos that's when it might get embarrassin'
Cos she knew for a fact who his father was
It was some soldiers from Catterick Garrison

Now before all the others could ask her an'all
She was saved by a ring on the bell
She says "Here hold the bairn, there's someone at the door"
And she jumped up to get it hersel'

And there stood this bloke in a gabardine mac
And a serious look on his face
He says "I'm looking for the woman that lives here"
Cissie says "Aye, well you're at the right place"

He says "I'm doing the Census, I'm here to take names
Of all the people that lives in this house
And he took out a pencil from the back of his lug
And says "Right, start wi' you and your spouse"

"No spouse," says Cissie, "Just me and our Wayne,
And there's Wayne and there's Wayne and there's Wayne"
But before she said more, the bloke at the door
Says "How come they've all got the same name?"

She says "It makes life a lot easier and I'll tell you for why,
When I want them in quick, do you see?
I shout 'Wayne' nice and loud and the whole bloody crowd,
Comes running to see what's for tea"

"It saves me remembering a whole load of names,
A daughter, eleven sons and three cats"
He thought for a while and he had to agree
It was pretty sound thinking, was that

Then he says "Hang about, that's all very well"
Then he got himself thinking some more
He says "What if you want them just one at a time?"
She says "That's what their surnames are for!"

'Owt For A Duck?

I was down at the Dole last Tuesday at ten
Signing on and trying me luck
I was searching the boards for a decent paid job
When the door opens and in walks a duck

He had his wife with two twins in a pushchair
Dead bold like nowt was amiss
And he sat them down safe in the waiting room
He says "Just wait here" and he gave her a kiss

So his missus picked up an old 'Woman's Realm'
And she started to thumb through the pages
Then she turned to the bairns and said "Just go to sleep,
It looks like your dad'll be ages"

Well there was a few people looked but no one said nowt
And the duck took his place in the queue
Then this lad turns around says "Bloody hell, you're a duck"
And the duck says "What's it to you?"

Then he got to the front and he sat at the desk
Mind, he'd to jump to get on the chair
The lad laughed and said "Shucks, we've got nowt for ducks"
Duck says "You've not even looked. That's not fair"

Well the lad on the desk, his jaw it just dropped
He says "Bloody hell, a duck that can speak,
Hang on and I'll get me supervisor down"
He says "Cos I've only been here a week"

Well the supervisor was out back on his teabreak
So he comes and says "What's going on?"
He says to the duck "What you doing on that chair?"
The duck says "Nowt, I've just come to sign on"

So the supervisor says "Hey, theres a talking duck here"
And the lad says "I know, I just said"
And the duck said "This is getting tedious"
And at that the two blokes went quite red

So the supervisor said "Sorry, didn't mean to be rude,
But you must realise we were taken aback,
We've had no training to deal with ducks that can talk,
You get used to them just going quack"

Then he says "No, this is great. My first talking duck,
I'll get you employment no bother,
Just give us your name and address on this form,
And pop back and see us tomorrow"

So the duck signed the form and bid them good day
Then he went to tell his wife what was said
But her and the bairns were surrounded with blokes
That were chucking them bits of stale bread

She says "How did it go?" He says "I've got to come back"
She says "Could they not find you nothing at all?"
And one of the blokes that was chucking the bread
Says "Bugger me, his wife talks an' all"

So she puts down the mag and she picks up her bag
They waddled out through the doors to go home
But before they'd got into the car park
The supervisor gets on the phone

He says "Wait till the newspapers hear about this,
There'll be no end of jobs for that duck,
He says "Eeh, I'm excited, might even get knighted"
His imagination was running amok

I couldn't stay away, I was down the next day
Just to see if the duck got a job
But you could hardly get in for reporters
It had attracted a right bloody mob

There's the supervisor sitting and looking dead smug
With a great big self-satisfied grin
He had a clean shirt and tie for the cameras
And he was waiting for the duck to come in

Well the duck family didn't know what the fuss was about
When they pushed the pushchair through the door
And when the twins saw the crowd they started to cry
And the cameras just flashed even more

So the supervisor rushed up and took the ducks wing
He says "Come in Mr Mallard, sit down,
I've talked to me colleagues and we've got you fixed up,
We've got you the best job in town"

He says "There's quite a demand for a duck that can talk,
But this'll send shivers down your spine,
There's a job with the Moscow State Circus,
You can start there tomorrow at nine"

But the duck looked confused he said "Hang on a mo,
I don't want you to think I'm a thicky,
But what do the Moscow State Circus want,
With me ...a qualified brickie?"

Deaf Wish

It was miserable that night in the Riveters Arms
Joviality? There wasn't a hint
Dick and Ted got their beers chalked up on account
On account of them both being skint

Another week without winning the domino
The pools? a complete waste of time
They sat there discussing their fortunes
And thought about turning to crime

They talked about Davy MacWalter
And his compensation bid
He'd put in for 'Industrial Deafness'
And got a pay-off of twelve thousand quid

"Thirty years in that noisy old shipyard,
We could hardly hear ourselves think,
We could say we'd gone deaf and put in a claim,
It wouldn't half kick up a stink!"

So they saw Ralphy Robson, the Union bloke
When they got to the yard that next morn'
He reluctantly went through the motions
And made them fill in loads of forms

Then they practised that night at the Riveters'
And ignored folks that called out their names
Their conversation was scattered with 'Pardon?'
'You what?' and the odd 'Come again?'

A few weeks passed and they both got a letter
To say that a date had been made
For them to go to the Doc's for a check-up
That would decide if they were going to get paid

Dick went in first to the Doctor
"Shut the door and sit down" the Doc said
So Dick shut the door and went for the chair
But the Doctor was shaking his head

He says "Sorry, bonny lad, you just dropped yourself in,
You just heard what I said loud and clear,
You're not really deaf, you're just pulling my leg,
You've got no right at all to be here"

Dick cursed and went back to the waiting room
And he had a quick word with old Ted
"Watch yourself mate, there's a stunt that he pulls,
To see if you heard what he said"

"Be careful when first you go in there,
He had me banged to rights straight away!
If he says 'shut the door' just don't do it,
In fact, don't do owt that he says"

So when Ted went through to the Doctor
He was putting some books on the shelf
He turned and said "Just shut the door please"
Ted says "Shut the bugger yourself!"

Norman's Bull

"Now then, says Bill, how you doing wi' that bull?
You were saying like it wouldn't perform,
Is it doing the business, earning its keep?"
"I'll tell you what happened," said Norm

"I was telling the vet'nary last week at the mart,
And he said he would come have a look,
So he came the next morn got his stethoscope out,
Then had a quick look in his book"

"He searched in his bag and he gave him some pills"
He says "Two twice a day for a week,
His van was hardly out of the yard,
When I heard this loud sort of shriek"

"So I turned and I looked and I nearly passed out,
The bull leapt the gate and he'd flew,
Right up the field where he serviced six cows,
A donkey, a horse and four ewes"

"In less than two days he'd been through the full herd,
And made a good job of it too,
So I lent him to Archie, up over the hill,
If you need him you'd best join the queue"

"There's no stopping him now, he's the talk of the mart,
Whatever it was in those pills,
They worked wonders at getting him going"
"So what were they called, then?" says Bill

"Well I'm not really sure, it was a long Latin name,
I should've written it down just in case,
But they're a big sort of round, pinky, tablet,
And they've a nice sort of peppermint taste"

The Ninth Hole

I'll tell you what happened to a mate of me dad's
Well he was more of a friend of a friend
Actually he hardly knew him at all
Just he lived two doors down from our Ken's

Ken's an uncle - least that's what we call him
He's not a real uncle, you know
He's just a bloke that me Dad used to work with
Anyway, it was him that knew this bloke Joe

He was a golfer this bloke, dead keen, all the gear
Played a round every day if he could
He had a handicap apparently, means nowt to me
But to golfers it seems it's quite good

He always did well all the way round the course
Till he got alongside Haggies Burn
It was the ninth hole and it proved a real problem
Par three with a bit of a turn

With the woods really tight along one side
And the river close by on the other
No matter how much he lined up his shot
He always got into bother

It was the same every time he got to the tee
His stomach it started to churn
Cos he knew no matter how hard he tried
He would slice the ball into the burn

He would practice his swing any time that he could
It was straight as a die, it would seem
But as soon as he got to the tee at the ninth
He would whack it straight into the stream

He got videos and books, took lessons and that
From this bloke that went out with his daughter
His confidence was high when he got to the ninth
But the ball always went in the water

Now his golfing improved he could really play well
He'd a swing of great style and panache
But when he got to the ninth it all went to pot
He'd close his eyes and wait for the splash

This phenomenon continued the rest of his life
No matter how hard the bloke tried
He kept knocking the ball in the river
Right up till the day that he died

In his will he said he wanted cremated
And his ashes scattered on the fairway
So his wife complied with his wishes
And took the urn up the course the next day

She walked round the course and found somewhere nice
The ninth fairway just past the turn
She said a short prayer and opened the lid
Then the ashes blew into the burn

He Was Always Dead Clever, Me Dad

We could never play football on Mondays
Our lane had all washing hung out
So we were just heading off to the river instead
When me Mother come and give us a shout

She says "Give us a hand, Son. Me washing's come down,
The hook in the wall's come unstuck,
I'm in a right flap cos the prop's gone and snapped,
And me sheets are all covered in muck"

I thought like me Dad would cos he'd sort it out
Then I tied up the line to nextdoor's
And me Mam got her purse and she gave us ten bob
To get a new prop at the Stores

Course, there's me never bought a new clothes prop before
But the man in the shop was quite good
He said "Beech was the best but cost more than the rest"
To me it was just a bit wood

I had such a job getting it out of the shop
What with it being three times me own size
I knocked two tins of yacht varnish off the top shelf
And poked this old bloke in the eye

Carrying a clothes prop the full length of the High Street
Proved to be yet another ordeal
And the Butchers lad, Mike, went and fell off his bike
When it got stuck in the spokes of his wheel

It was me mother that noticed the mistake I had made
As soon as I got back from the shop
Course, I wasn't big enough to see the far end
And there wasn't a vee at the top

What would Dad do? He'd sort it out
So I went and I found his big saw
But of course, I was nowhere near tall enough
So I borrowed a ladder from nextdoor

I leaned the ladder against the wall of the yard
And wedged the prop in the flags by the door
Then I climbed up and marked where it had to be cut
Then I climbed back on down for the saw

I was ready to climb back up to the top
When the gate opens and in comes me Dad
He says "That looks queer, what's going on here?"
So I told him the plan that I had

He says "Don't be so daft" and he stood there and laughed
"Do they not teach you nothing at school?"
He says "Give us that saw. Now just watch yer Pa"
So I watched and I felt such a fool

He's dead brainy, me Dad, He says "Righto, me lad
You don't need the ladder no more"
Then he stuck one end of the prop in the ground
Went in the house and shut the back door

Then he opened the back bedroom window
He says "Hang on tight, there's a good lad"
Grabbed hold of the prop, sawed a vee in the top
He was always dead clever, me Dad!

The Plodgeborough And District Volunteer Fire Brigade

There's a farm up ower yon top side
That's all wheat fields and barley and that
It's got acres and acres of turnips
And it's owned by Lord Proglington-Matt

Now old Cecil Maughan was bringing in corn
Slap bang in the middle o' the crop
The corn was as high as an elephant's eye
When his tractor suddenly spluttered and stopped

He'd had bother with his fuel pipe all morning
Kept coming off and driving him mad
But this time it come off, there was a dirty great whuff
And the whole bloody thing took a ha'ad

There was flames licking all round the paintwork
Burning petrol all ower the shop
And with a wind from the north blowin for all it was worth
It soon took a ha'ad to the crop

Now, Lord Proglington-Matt had just tied his cravat
And lifted the latch on his door
He was just leaving the house to bag a few grouse
Impervious to what the day had in store

Then his lungs filled wi' smoke and he started to choke
As he looked and saw what was gan' on
So he shouts to his maid "Phone the Fire Brigade"
Which was daft, cos there isn't a one

Well, there isn't as such, but she looked at her watch
And phoned the Riveters' to speak to her Dad
She says "Tell the volunteers to put down their beers,
Lord Prog's bottom field's caught a ha'ad"

So her dad shouts for Joe to give the siren a blow
Thus alerting the rest of the crew
They all ran up the woods where the fire truck was stood
And had been since before World War Two

Now in charge of the mob was Benny the Gob
A fully-qualified hoover repairman
And second in command was the Kleeneze man
Who was also part-time Concert Chairman

They booled the truck down from the top of the hill
The engine spluttered and burst into life
And through a cloud of blue smoke, on jumped eight blokes
Two Girl Guides and the Minister's wife

They were a right motley crew but they'd just have to do
And with old Jessop ringing the bell
They flew out of the town trying not to slow down
Cos they needed a good run at the hill

But when they reached the long drag up towards Stotty Crag
They all had to jump off and get pushing
Benny the gob wasn't chuffed cos they ran out of puff
And sat there pantin' and gaspin' and blushing

Inch by inch they reached the brow of the hill
And they jumped back on board and held tight
And as it bombed down the slope they just had to hope
That the fire would still be alight

Now Mr Wallace the Polis had seen all the smoke
And had pedalled ower there on his bike
He found Lord Prog and his dog just stood there agog
Never ever having seen nowt of the like

They heard the fire engine approaching
Tyres screeching as it rounded the turn
It didn't slow down it drove straight through the gate
And smacked the tractor right into the burn

It sent up such a splash that the field was awash
And it drownded out most of the blaze
There was just a bit trouble with a few bits of stubble
And Cecil's pants which'd seen better days

But that valiant crew knew just what to do
And they stamped and they beat at the flames
Minister's wife, Mrs Hardy, beat them out with her cardy
While the lads grabbed the hose and took aim

Now their big tank of watter, having took such a clatter
Decided to burst at the seams
It sent a dirty great shower o' watter all ower
And what was left of the fire turned to steam

"That's just the job" says Benny the gob
Dick and Ted says "Aye, very nice,
Just as well I suppose, you seen the state of this hose?
It's full of holes on account of the mice"

Up goes a shout "That's it, the fire's out"
Lord Proggy runs up, mind, was he chuffed
His face was aglow he shouts "Bloody good show,
You chaps really do know your stuff"

"I'm going to make a donation of five hundred pounds"
And he wrote out a cheque there and then
And Benny the gob muttered "Aye, just the job"
Dick and Ted said "Very nice" once again

Benny yelps with delight "We'll get flashing blue light,
And that engine's as flat as a fart,
And now the water tank's burst but first things come first,
We'll get them brakes bloody fixed for a start!"

Twelve Days

Sid Brocklebank's got the junk shop down Bolsover Street
And there's nowt he hasn't got there, I'll bet
From ex-army teeth, to a side of corned beef
And owt he's not got he can get

He was in his window one day putting stuff on display
And he noticed this well dressed looking chap
Not a local, the bloke, stood there having a smoke
He wore a trilby not just a cap

Sid gave him a nod and went back to his job
And thought no more about it, till when
The ding-dong thing on his door went ping
And there stood the bloke once again

He says "Is that a partridge you've got in the window?"
Sid says "Aye, you're in luck, me last one,
It's yours for ten bob." Bloke says "Aye, just the job,
If you throw in that perch that it's on"

"That's no perch, isn't that" says our Sid with a snap
"That's a genuine pear tree stood there,
Tell you what, though" says Sid, "Take them both for a quid"
"Okay," says the bloke, "That sounds fair"

"It's for the woman I love, don't suppose you keep doves?
A nice pair of white ones would do"
Sid says "Are turtle ones all right? They're not really white,
They're more of a speckly hue"

"Smashin" he says, "Now, what about hens?"
Sid says "Hens?" He says "Aye, she likes eggs"
"I've French ones, there's three, and they're plump as can be,
They're just a bit short in the legs"

He says "Can they sing?" Sid says "Sing? Hens don't sing,
They just squawk and drive everyone potty,
But I've four calling birds, sweetest singers you've heard,
They can sing like that bloke Pavarotti"

Sid says "I've not heard of a lass liking birds,
Instead of daft jewellery and things"
The bloke says "That reminds me, thanks very much,
I'll have five of them shiny gold rings"

He got his eyes on Sid's geese and says "Giz half a dozen"
Like as if they were going out of fashion
"How's about seven swans?" "Eeh you're having us on?
I'll have them an all." Sid says "Smashing"

Then he noticed the cows that Sid kept out the back
Sid says "No, put your wallet away"
He says, "I'm not going to sell, cos there's milkmaids as well,
I'd have to give them redundancy pay"

He bought the milkmaids, the lot, he'd buy owt, like as not
So Sid thought that he'd just chance his arm
And see how much more he could get him to spend
Well, being greedy doesn't do any harm

He says "Here's an idea that'll bring her some cheer,
And a one that might just make her day,
There's about nine Scottish pipers practising upstairs,
For a few beers, they might come round and play"

The bloke shouted hooray, he said 'yes' straight away
And his eyeballs lit up like a kid
He says "That would be swell, can you get dancers as well,
And I'll throw in another few quid?"

So he got him ten lasses from Miss Bollard's dance classes
He says "Can you get us some male dancers too?"
So he booked him a dozen 'Lords-a-leaping'
But there was one of 'em down with the flu

There was a drummers' convention up at the Town Hall
And as soon as the bloke heard the racket
He says "Ring the Town Hall and book that lot an' all?"
Sid says "What? It'll cost you a packet!"

He says "Money's no object but I think that's me lot,
I don't want folks thinking I'm daft"
Sid says "Oh well, righto. You started it though"
And the bloke looked at Sid and just laughed

He says "No, that's me lot, lets have a look what we've got,
Now I don't want to take them away,
I'd like them delivered to my girlfriend's address,
But not all to arrive the same day"

Sid wasn't too keen, he says "How d'you mean?"
He says "Send round the partridge tomorrow,
And the day after that, the two turtle doves,
Then the French hens the next, do you follow?"

"The day after that, there's the four calling birds,
And the rings on the following day,
Then the geese and the swans and whole carry-on..."
Sid says "Whoa lad, hang on. There's no way"

"I mean, I'm really obliged for your order n'that,
Like anyone, I could do with the business,
But they'll stay on the shelf unless you take 'em yourself,
......Cos I'm closed for twelve days over Christmas"

Joey Ruddick's Bad Foot

He was a shy little budgie Joey Ruddick
A man of few words you might say
'Sod off' were two of his favourites, I'm told
'Part from that he'd sit quiet all day

One evening, on his fly round the parlour
He went up to the window and looked out
And a dirty great moth, one of them four-engine jobs
Was rattling the glass with its snout

"I'll chin you, you great fairy" thought Joey
"You and whose army?" the moth asked
So they both hovered back for a couple of feet
Then they both stuck the nut on the glass

They carried on in that manner for ten minutes or more
Not quite grasping the concept of windows (Windahs)
Until Joey was that dizzy he fell into the hearth
And burnt his foot on a hot bit of cinders

The vet'nary, Mr Gough, had a look the next day
It wasn't the worst foot he'd seen
And he told Ruby "You'll soon make it better,
If you bathe it with dilute iodine"

Ruby went straight to the Co-operative chemist
With a crisp ten-bob note in her hand
She couldn't see any iodine made by 'Dilutes'
So she had to get the Co-op's own brand

She religiously bathed it for almost two weeks
With neat iodine and a clean bit of cloth
Until the strangest of things went and happened
Joey's foot shrivelled up and dropped off

You could see Joey wasn't too tickled
He said "Agh yah!" and then went in a grump
He couldn't believe when he looked in his mirror
His mate too, had one leg and a stump

When Leonard the Lodger came in from the pit
Seeing Joey said "It wouldn't take much,
Just two or three matchsticks and some fuse wire,
I could make the poor bugger a crutch"

So he set-to that very same evening
And fashioned a crutch like he'd said
And he fastened it to Joey's right oxter
With the fusewire wrapped twice round his head

Joey felt a right narna stood there with a crutch
You could see by the look on his face
But his mate in the mirror had got one an'all
So he didn't feel too out of place

Now as with most budgies the floor of his cage
Was all sandpaper for in order to scratch
When he hopped down that night his crutch set alight
Cos the red end had been left on the match

The vet'nary, Mr Gough said "The smell would soon go,
And not to worry about him being a bit black"
He gave them some cream for where the feathers had been
And assured them, "One day, they'll grow back"

Joey was straight up his ladder as soon as he got home
To the mirror and have a winge to his mate
He saw what looked like a baldy old spuggy
That had suffered a similar fate

"Who's a pretty boy?" he chirped, just to cheer the lad up
It seemed to work cos he said the same back
Joey says "Eeh, look at you!" He says "Eeh look at you!"
And they stood and they had a bit crack

Just then Leonard the lodger put his hand in the cage
And Joey took a chunk out his thumb
He'd this notion to make Joey a prosthetic foot
From a pipe cleaner and a bit chewing gum

Joey wasn't having none of it, he pecked and he squawked
Shouting "Sod off" he pecked down to the bone
Until Ruby comes through, she says "What's going on?"
Leonard says "I think I'll just leave him alone"

Now there's only so much a budgie can stand
Joey was reaching the end of his tether
He packed up his mirror, his ladder and bell
And his ointment to rub on his feathers

And that night on his fly round the parlour
He got on top of the pelmet and hid
And Ruby shouts "Eeeh. Where the hell can he be?"
And Leonard says "Well I never did!"

"Must've gone up the chimley while we watched The Glums,
Poor lad'll've got such a fright,
He'll be all sooty and black, but he'll find his way back,
So we'll leave open that window tonight"

They've never seen nowt more of Joey since then
But I've heard that he's doing all right
Cos some twitchers reported a bird with one foot
Seen chasing a moth, Sunday night

So if you see a baldy spuggy in your garden
And you hear a faint budgie's bell ringing
It's probably Joey Ruddick from Bolsover Street
Especially if it's 'Sod off' he's singing

The Bethlehem Charabanc Trip

Me Auntie Barbara's son Joe lives down our back row
And he was telling us about Mary, his bird
And the morning of the Bethlehem charabanc trip
He said the funniest of things had occurred

Mary, his fiancée, had just left their Nancy's
When there happened the most strangest of things
There was a puff of white smoke and there stood this bloke
In a nightie with a halo and wings

Well she jumped with the fright, she says "You've no right,
Putting the willies up people like that,
I've come ower all queer, I'm all wobbly stood here,
I'll have to sit down you daft pratt"

He says "I'm sorry for the fright, it's Mary, am I right?
I've got summat in here, just for you,
From our Lord God Almighty" he put his hand in his nightie
Mary went a bit faint and said "Ooh!"

She was relieved, poor soul, when he pulled out a scroll
Started to read about joy and glad tidings
She says "You'd best sling your harp and bugger off sharp,
Cos if our Joe comes you'll get a good hiding"

"Hang on Mrs er…, It's all 'whyfores' and 'wheres'"
She says "Miss!" He says "What?" She says "Miss!"
"Miss?" he says "Oh, you're not married?" She says "No"
He says "In that case it's bad news, is this"

He says "What it says, is in a couple of days,
Your going to give birth to a saviour,
Some sort of Messiah" She says "Eeh, you big liar,
We don't go in for that sort of behaviour"

Mary was struck dumb, then as fast as he'd come
He done a bunk in a flash of white light
She says "O yeah, thanks a bunch, put us right off me lunch,
And now me corsets have gone really tight"

She met up with her pals down by the canal
Where the charabanc was sat sitting waitin'
"What time d'you call this?" said Joe givin her a kiss
She says "Shush, Joe, give ower creatin'"

Joe helped her on the bus, made a right flaming fuss
Gave a heave and gritted his teeth
He gave a big push, Mary started to blush
He says "Bugger me, you've n'arf piled on some beef"

"Shut yer gob, Joe. There's summat you should know,
I've just discovered I'm gan' to give birth"
He looked straight in her eye "You what?" She says "Aye"
And started explaining for all she was worth

He says "I'm supposin' we should be glad we were chosen,
Fancy picking us! What's the odds?
There's summat I'm missin, d'you get pregnant by kissin?"
She says "No, you daft tatie, it's God's"

She thought she'd best mention divine intervention
Cos Joe was, like, smelling a rat
He says "Oh aye, hunky-dory, you mean he takes the glory,
And leaves us with the bairn, bugger that!"

It was quite a long drive and by the time they arrived
The whole bus was all laughing and shrieking
But at the back of the bus things were needing discussed
And by this time Joe and Mary weren't speaking

After a day on the booze, Joe was singin the blues
Well actually, he was joining in wi' 'Wild Rover'
Mary grabbed at his hand, she says "I don't feel too grand,
I think you and me'd best stop over"

After they'd piled all the gang back on Bill's Charabanc
They went wandering the streets for a bed
And at quarter to three, they found a cheap B&B
But "I'm sorry, we're full up" the bloke said

"I've got no rooms" he said "But I've got this bit shed,
It's quite dry and there's plenty hay in it"
Mary shouts "That'll do" and then she went "Ooh!"
She says "Me contractions are every three minutes!"

Bloke says "Hang on a tick, I know a shepherd called Mick,
He's a dab hand at lambing and that,
He'll know what to do, I've seen him wi' ewes,
And he helped Mrs Nicholson's cat"

It was early that morn' that the baby was born
Then three wise men from the west wandered in
They said "For summat so young, he's a fine pair of lungs,
You can hear it a mile away, that din"

One of 'em had a runny nose and when he came close
He looked like Persian or Mesopotamian
Just then he sneezes and Mary shouts "Jesus!"
Joe says "Write that down, it's better than Damien"

While wiping his eyes Joe says "That's not too wise,
You could give the poor bugger your cold"
He says "No, yer okay, I'm just allergic to hay"
Then he handed over a bag full of gold

Joe says "That's very kind - are you sure you don't mind?
Thanks a lot, hey, this isn't too bad"
He looked at Mary and kid and said "Well I never did,
I could get used to this being a dad"

He says "It's brilliant is this" he gave Mary a kiss
And went off to phone Auntie Barbara
Thinking, "Bethlehem's quite nice but I'll not do this twice,
Next year we're going to Scarborough"